POWER DADS

POWER DADS

A User-Friendly Manual for Better Fathering

CHARLES M. SELL

CARTOON AND ACTION STEPS BY
T. W. AYERS

VINE BOOKS

Servant Publications
Ann Arbor, Michigan

© 1996 by Charles M. Sell and T. W. Ayers
All rights reserved.

Vine Books is an imprint of Servant Publications especially designed to serve evangelical Christians.

All Scripture quotations, unless indicated, are taken from the HOLY BIBLE, NEW INTERNATIONAL VERSION® © 1973, 1978, 1984 by International Bible Society. Used by permission of Zondervan Publishing House. All rights reserved.

Published by Servant Publications
P.O. Box 8617
Ann Arbor, Michigan 48107

Cover design: Eric Walljasper

96 97 98 99 00   10 9 8 7 6 5 4 3 2 1

Printed in the United States of America
ISBN 0-89283-979-1

LIBRARY OF CONGRESS CATALOGING-IN-PUBLICATION DATA

Sell, Charles M.
  Power dads : a user-friendly manual for better fathering / Charles M. Sell ; cartoon and action steps by T.W. Ayers.
    p. cm.
  Includes bibliographical references (p.   ).
  ISBN 0-89283-979-1
   1. Fatherhood. 2. Fatherhood—Religious aspects—Christianity. I. Ayers, T.W. (Timothy Wayne). II. Title.
HQ756.S44 1996
306.874'2—dc20   96-29011
                                                                CIP

CONTENTS

Part One: Wise Father

1. Realize the Need / 11
   Nonessential You're Not

2. Picture the Role (Part 1) / 17
   Doing the Dad Thing

3. Picture the Role (Part 2) / 23
   Doing the Dad Thing

4. Recognize the Rewards / 29
   The Payoff Is Unlike Any Other

5. Face Your Fear / 35
   Beware the Paranoid Parent Syndrome

6. Be Consistent / 41
   Be It Again, Dad

7. Deal with Your Past / 47
   To Be a Dad, First Be a Son

8. Tap into the Power Source / 55
   When You're Weak, You're Strong

Part Two: Able Man

9. Be Always Changing / 67
   Make the Long Trip from Head to Habit

10. Manage Anger / 73
    The One Who Makes You Angry May Be You

11. Accept Conflict / 83
    Add Conflict to Taxes and Death
12. Plan Your Life / 91
    Manage Your Life or It Will Manage You

Part Three: Capable Companion

13. See the Value of Conversation / 101
    Talk May Be Cheap, but It's Valuable
14. Try Talking / 109
    Finding the Lost Art of Conversation
15. Learning to Listen / 115
    How to See with Your Ears
16. Understand How Kids Think / 123
    Little Adults They're Not

Part Four: Spiritual Teacher

17. Be the Spiritual Leader / 131
    Build a Solid Foundation
18. Shape a Child's Values and Teach Informally / 139
    Cooperate with Your Kid's Best Teacher
19. Create Rituals / 147
    Welcoming God into the Kitchen
20. Conduct Family Devotions / 155
    A Contemporary Design for the Family Altar

Part Five: Competent Trainer

21. Observe the Guidelines / 163
    Discipline As You Are Disciplined
22. Discipline by Natural Consequences / 169
    Enroll Your Kid in the School of Hard Knocks

23. Use Behavior Modification / 177
    A Positive Approach to the Negative

24. Consider Spanking / 183
    Does the Carrot Make the Stick Obsolete?

25. Avoid Dominating / 191
    Use Your Urge to Control on Yourself

26. Help Your Child Differentiate / 199
    Teach Your Kid to Fly

27. Empower / 207
    Be a Support, Not a Substitute

"Power Dads is insightful without being pedantic, and readable without being superficial. This is a logical, common sense approach to being a better father. It doesn't rely on gimmicks, hyperbole, or strained analogies. Instead, it was lovingly written by a couple of guys who have—apparently—been there."

—ROBERT DARDEN
Author of *The Way of an Eagle,* and editor of the world's oldest and largest (and only) religious humor and satire magazine, *The Door.*

PART ONE

WISE FATHER

Dad, you?

ONE

REALIZE THE NEED

Nonessential You're Not

POWER VERSE
So God created man in his own image, in the image of God he created him; male and female he created them.   GENESIS 1:27

POWER LESSON
Derek Redmond wanted to make it to the finish line. This was possibly one of those chances of a lifetime. He might never again run in the semifinal of a 400-meter Olympic race. Yet, the chances of this British runner's making it were slim. More than halfway into the race, a torn hamstring rendered one leg useless. Running was impossible; he could hardly walk. Determined to cross the line, he hobbled onward, the grimace on his face and his awkward gait signaling that each step was agonizingly painful. The sympathetic crowd cheered him on, fearing he would give up and collapse on the dirt.

Suddenly, a man ran out of the stands toward the track. Avoiding the security guard's efforts to stop him, he reached the struggling athlete. When he grabbed him around the waist, Derek slung his arm across his shoulders. While the crowd cheered and millions throughout the world watched on television, Derek Redmond finished the race, supported by his father.

This touching father-son drama from the 1992 Olympics was broadcast on television over and over again. Had it been his coach or his mother or a friend, the effect would have been different. Not that a man doesn't need his mother's backing or that she is any less important than his dad in any way. It's just that a father and mother are different.

God is responsible for this difference. Males and females are created in God's image. While they are equal in value and in many ways very similar, they are not the same. As they each play a crucial role in a child's life, their roles are somewhat distinctive.

Fatherless in America

Recent research is showing us just how crucial it is for a child to have a father around the house, or at least to have a man in his or her life. Yet, some people deny this, as Dan Quayle's controversy with Murphy Brown revealed. He criticized this TV character's decision to have a baby and raise it without a father, and was mercilessly castigated by some people.

About the same time, an article in the *Washington Post* stated that some social scientists had concluded that the consequences of the absence of fathers in the home were overstated and that the two-parent household was far less critical to the healthy development of children than previously believed.[1]

In his book *Fatherless America,* David Blankenhorn points out that this viewpoint often shows up in comments made by so-called experts. As an example, he points to their analysis of the case of a troubled teenager, Joseph Chancy, Jr., who made the front page of the *Wall Street Journal* when he was arrested in Miami and charged with the crime of robbery. Though only thirteen years old, he was ordered by the grand jury to be tried as an adult. Joseph's mother, Yvonne Jackson, was thirty-six years old, had never married, and has three sons, each by a different man. None of the boys ever really knew his father. This prompted numerous discussions of the cause of violent juvenile crime. Among them were access to guns, involvement in gangs and mobs, exposure to violence in the mass media, lack of parental supervision, physical punishment, substance abuse, social and economic inequality, prejudice and discrimination, and lack of anti-violence programs and psychological services in schools and communities. Yet, Blankenhorn says, they never mentioned that one of the causes might have been the absence of Joseph Chancy, Sr.[2]

Many social scientists strongly believe the lack of a father in a child's life is a major cause of problems for today's children, and they have a heap of research to back them up. Barbara Whitehead used those research findings for an article in the prestigious *Atlantic Monthly* to confirm that Dan Quayle was right.[3]

The more we study the role of fathers, the more we see how important it is. Just as kids need vitamins to be physically healthy, so they need contact with dad (or a male substitute) to be psychologically healthy. And a kid suffers from dad deficiency just as he does from a lack of vitamins. The absence of fathers may be as damaging to the home as the absence of mothers. And the damage is considerable—to the child and to society.

Blankenhorn has convincingly pictured what happens to children who grow up in fatherless homes. They are five times more likely to live in poverty than children who live in homes with fathers. They are more subject to sexual abuse—from their mothers' boyfriends or outsiders. Their schoolwork suffers; they're not only more likely to be lower achievers, but their chances of being expelled or suspended increase. And they will more likely be delinquent and have trouble with the police. That they end up being more violent is conspicuous to anyone who knows anything about criminals in America. A one-parent family is a better predictor of a person's involvement in crime than either race or economic status. Too many boys have guns because they don't have fathers.[4] The physical absence of a father for as much as a year seems to be connected with the incidence of delinquency.

Emotional problems are more probable for single-parent kids than those in two-parent homes, and they'll more frequently be found in a counselor's office. Having a sense of personal self-esteem and identity will be a struggle for them. The statistics here are impressive and alarming.

Though the cause of homosexuality is still a mystery, one factor for some homosexual men is that they had absent or cold and detached fathers.[5] Sixty-seven percent of boys with sex-role problems were not living in a home with their biological father. The more profoundly disturbed the boy is in sex-role adjustment, the more likely he is to be separated from his biological father.[6] *It appears that a father is more important to a son's and daughter's male and female role than a mother is.*

Many boys growing up without close male examples often become one of two extreme types of men. They are homosexual or they are macho. Unable to figure out what a man should be like, they either retreat or they act out the typical tough guy image. This is coupled with a dislike for females, an underlying rage against them, sometimes driving young men to violent acts against women.

Turn these statistics around and you can begin to see what having a man around the house means to children—as well as to women and society in general. For this reason, single mothers should do their best to keep their children in touch with their fathers, when possible, or else they should provide them close contact with other men.

We fathers need to recognize how badly our kids need us.

Statistically speaking, if we are there for our children, they will have a higher standard of living, do better at school, be less likely to commit any crime, be more emotionally stable, and more sure of their sexual identity. That should be enough to make any of us want to hang around the house and learn to be good at fathering.

POWER ACTIONS

Starting tomorrow and continuing for one week, keep track of the hours you spend at home, at work, and at outside events. Sleeping doesn't count, and that includes naps after dinner. Where does family time fall in the big three? Can it be improved any? Is every meeting you go to that important?

Look at your calendar. Is there a week when you can be home every evening? If not, do as many of the seven days as possible. While you are home, play with the kids. Assist with homework. Watch their favorite shows. When they're grown, you can't get those lost days back.

If you are separated or divorced and your kids aren't with you every day, you can be available to them, but you have to be creative. Send cards. Call often. Let them know that you are an active, involved dad even though you don't live with them. But all of that depends on your having a good relationship with your ex-wife. Ask yourself, "Are my kids worth my making a gesture of peace?"

"It looks like it's Dad's night to cook again."

T W O

PICTURE THE ROLE (PART 1)

Doing the Dad Thing

POWER VERSE
A good man leaves an inheritance for his children's children.
PROVERBS 13:22

POWER LESSON
Not all men realize how much kids need a dad to hang out with. Apparently the wealthy J. Paul Getty didn't. He made a fortune in fossil fuels but "showed his five sons all the warmth of a dinosaur.... Too busy making millions, he skipped the weddings, births, operations, and even funerals of his children and grandchildren."[1]

Like Getty, many fathers seem to have little idea what a dad means to a child. This, in part, keeps them from investing time and effort into being a dad. Men who dedicate themselves to their kids do so because they know how critical their involvement is.

Though we can't be absolutely sure about the distinctive contribution a father makes to a child's life, there are some things about which we can be fairly certain. The first is as profound as it is important: fathers contribute a male presence to their families. Just being there makes a difference.

I learned about the impact of presence when I was a hospital chaplain. There were times when it was difficult to do much for someone in distress. When parents watched their child die or when a patient was too sick to talk or listen, there was little I could do or say to help. Yet, I could still minister to them—by my presence. My name tag identified me as a representative of God. Without a word, I signified to people the existence of a spiritual realm where strength, meaning, and comfort could ease their distress. To convey this didn't depend on what I was feeling or thinking. I was playing a role which was often extremely important to distressed people. To do that, all I had to do was be there.

Dad is a role we play, and we don't entirely write the script for it. A child gets all sorts of cues from many places about what dad means, and she knows it is good and significant. Thus, when you are at home or at the recital or in the backyard, you give her what she believes dad to be. When you are not there, she must deal with the loss of something she believes is important.

When I speak to groups of men, I often ask them what cherished memories they have of being with their fathers. Of course, they mention fishing, hunting, trips to ball games, and the like. It was doing them with dad that made them special. But some men turn negative, like one I remember. "My father was rarely in the stands when I played baseball. The few times he was there made me feel great; but because they were so few, I don't feel good about them now."

As this man spoke, I could see he was feeling a mixture of anger and remorse. A father's absence seems to cause as much pain as his presence does delight. Another man's comment highlighted that point. He said that one of his favorite things as a child was to study in the family room when his dad was there. He had no memories of conversation—his father was busy reading and they rarely talked. Yet, he remembers the warm, special feeling of being in the same room together.

Imagine that! Just being there can mean so much to your child. Where else can you do so much by just showing up?

Second, he is a leader. Many Christians question whether or not the Bible designates clear-cut roles for men and women in marriage. Instead of the husband leading and the wife submitting, they insist that Scripture teaches a mutual submission and that male and female are essentially the same in Christ.

Our space is too limited for us to argue a conclusion on this issue and still be fair to both sides. Rather, we want to simply claim that whether you are an egalitarian (no distinct husband-wife roles) or a complementarian (distinct roles), you have to conclude that the man should be a leader in his home—at least a co-leader. For one thing, fathers should lead their children. Children cannot be in charge. Fathers should co-parent with their wives and that means doing some leading. Egalitarians do not argue against shared leadership in the home. They do not say the wife should be the sole leader of the marriage. In my experience, most women today would be happy doing less leading. The modern husband may be more apt to abdicate a leadership position. Homes need leadership. A power vacuum, not a power struggle, exists in most homes. Women are forced into taking responsibility they often don't want. When men come home from work, they fall into a reclining chair rather than a throne. So, even if you believe both of you should be in charge, you, as a man, need to take leadership once in a while.

The traditional view of the man as the leader is not detrimental, as it's sometimes made out to be. Scripture never said that the man's being the head of the wife was a privileged position or that it rendered males and females unequal. Rather, the man's leadership is a grave responsibility, not an honor or badge of superiority. Headship is not a head trip.

Traditional leadership was to be done in love. "Wives, submit to your husbands as to the Lord. For the husband is the head of the wife as Christ is the head of the church, his body, of which he is the Savior. Now as the church submits to Christ, so also wives should submit to their husbands in everything. Husbands, love your wives, just as Christ loved the church and gave himself up for her" (Eph 5:22-25). Any husband who leads in this sacrificial way is not going to dominate his wife or disregard her needs, opinions, and dreams. Note, too, the passage never asks you to assume the leadership role by seizing power. Rather, it asks wives to submit to their husbands as to the Lord. If a wife chooses not to do that, no man can force her to; nor should he. On the other hand, no woman should dominate her family members and force them into submission to her will.

Christlike leadership requires taking the initiative in seeing things get done on schedule. It requires tackling problems, guiding the family to make decisions, and undertaking projects. It doesn't mean silencing other members, but rather listening to them and seeking their opinion and efforts.

Even if you think wives and mothers should also do this, it's clear that the husband-father should participate as well. Children need fathers who lead. There is some research evidence a child is likely to identify with the parent who is the leader in the household. Boys from homes in which the mother asserted herself as the leader exhibited more feminine sex-role preferences than boys from homes in which the father was leader.

The father is a protector. Though a mother also shields a child from harm, a man may offer a sense of security she can't. Although it is not always true, men are perceived to be strong, and that strength is associated with protection.

Men protect in a number of ways. One way is by disciplining their children. Some kids, especially rebellious boys, can be physically threatening to a mother. She is unable to keep them in line and needs a father to do so. This is why delinquent boys generally come from homes without a dad. A dad's discipline is a kind of protection. Without it, many kids end up dead or in prison.

On television, I heard a testimony of this protection from an unlikely source. Candice Bergen, who plays the part of TV's Murphy Brown, was being interviewed about her own father, the famous Edgar Bergen. "My dad saved me," she said. She explained that though he was a kind man, he was strict. Other actors' kids were spoiled, allowed to do anything, and given money and cars to do it. Many of them became drug addicts or otherwise ruined their lives. But because of her father, she did not. Protecting means preparing children for uncertain and potential future dangers.

Dads protect in other ways as well. They do it by being sensitive to their children's and wives' fears. Children and women are generally more afraid of being attacked than are men. Research shows that the category of women least worried about crime (young adult women) are still more worried about their personal safety than the most fearful group of men (over sixty-five).[2]

Since men are less fearful of their personal safety, they might not understand how their children may feel. The man around the house should honor his children's need for security and provide as best he can. He can agree to dead bolt locks, window bars, a security system, and whatever else is necessary to make his wife and children feel safe.

One of my vivid childhood memories is related to crossing a bridge near our home. Meant only for streetcars, the bridge had no walkway for pedestrians. We should not have used it to cross the stream. To cross we would have to step on the wooden ties that held the tracks. As we carefully stepped from tie to tie, we could peer through the two-foot gaps between them at the stony shallow river sixty feet below. It was always a frightening trip across the one-hundred-foot span. The only times I crossed without fear were when I was carried on my dad's shoulders. My mother's fear and constant warnings to my father to be careful are also part of the memory. All I recall is the feeling of security as I clutched my father's hair and felt his strong body beneath me. I recollect crossing that bridge as a special event, not a scary one. My dad was there to protect me.

POWER ACTIONS

Kids just naturally turn to their parents for protection. For them life is glutted with dangers and fears, but dad's being there makes it possible to face the scary parts of life. Respect your wife's and kids' fears. Do what you can to make them feel secure. Be the leader and protector they want you to be. Granted, power dads can't be all-powerful, but they can be all-caring.

THREE

PICTURE THE ROLE (PART 2)

Doing the Dad Thing

POWER VERSE

For you know that we dealt with each of you as a father deals with his own children, encouraging, comforting and urging you to live lives worthy of God.   1 THESSALONIANS 2:11

POWER LESSON

Providing is part of a father's protection. Families need to be shielded from poverty's hardships. Unfortunately, many men have forgotten this. Today we speak of the "feminization of poverty"; many women are unable to provide for their children without help from the fathers. Generally, divorce or marital separation means reduced income for women and higher income for men. Of all married-couple families in the nation in 1992 about 6 percent lived in poverty; of all female-headed families about 35 percent lived in poverty—a ratio of almost 6 to 1.[1]

Many fathers of the past felt their job was done when they brought home the paycheck. The need for a man to contribute economically to his family is as great today as it was then. Obviously, we men can't always provide as we would want to, but faithfulness is not measured by ability, but effort.

Giving Attention

Besides contributing to the family's finances, we men would do well to give priority to the so-called "little things" that need to be done around the house. Wives need more than love and romance from their men. And kids need more than food, clothes, and shelter. So says a very practical proverb, "Many a man claims to have unfailing love, but a faithful man who can find?" (Prv 20:6). Picture a husband showering his wife with amorous words about undying love that will go on and on and on, while she is thinking, "If only he'd fix the kitchen light switch!" Being someone to rely on for practical things is a major demonstration of love. Promptly fixing the kitchen light switch can mean a great deal to your wife, just as quickly fixing your kid's bike may be very special to your kid.

Yet, many of us men delay doing these things or fail to do them altogether. Perhaps what lies behind this failure is the tendency for us to take advantage of people who are closest to us. A man who fails to respond to his wife's plea to fix her car is often very quick to help others. Wives often complain to me that their husbands spend time repairing things in other people's homes, but take forever to get around to the broken things in their own home. It seems that we excuse ourselves for neglecting family by saying, "It's just a little thing." We think that if we do the "big" things, our family should put up with the little omissions. Another thought is: "You'll forgive me." We expect those close to us to go easy on us. However, it's OK to say, "I goofed, please forgive me." But it's not right to think, *"You'll forgive me, so I'll goof."* And then there's the "God wants me to put others first" thinking. Does he? Don't love and faithfulness begin at home? And finally, there's the "Words are enough" advantage-taker. "I wanted to fix your bike tonight, but my friend Jake came over and we got to talking." Or else, "I wanted to buy you something special for your birthday, but you know how busy I've been, so here's a plant I picked up at the grocery store." We think loved ones are supposed to be grateful for our good intentions and lame excuses. Why should they be? Families need more than promises; they need promise keepers.

Giving Affirmation

Dads need to be affirmers because kids need to be noticed. The family is baby's welcoming committee. What parents say and do makes a child feel it belongs in the family and the world. If a baby is abused and rejected, it will feel unwelcome, and that feeling may stick with the child throughout life. Said one thirty-something man who was abused as a child, "When I go to a party, I have this terrible feeling that someone is going to come up to me, tap me on the shoulder, and say, 'Will you get out of here? You don't belong.'"

Children who are loved and cherished will feel good about themselves. Their worth as a person and identity as a man or woman will be confirmed. Research shows that it is a father's affirmation that makes a young girl secure in her role as a woman. Though a daughter is made to feel good about her gender role by identifying with a mother who is secure, it seems to be the father's notice of her that is most crucial to the daughter's comfort in being a woman. It is because he is of the opposite sex that his approval of her as a girl means so much to her. This prepares her for the validation that other men, particularly her husband, will make in her life later. A dad must be prepared to react favorably to her. When she dons that new dress for her first big party, he needs to burst with pride and tell her how grown up and attractive she looks.

His nonsexual touch also means much to her. A father must

not make the mistake of physically withdrawing from her when she reaches her early teens. Many men stop hugging and touching their daughters because they are so afraid of a sexual gesture toward them. However, girls who grow up without affirming attention from their fathers (or some other father figure) often have serious gender identity problems. Research shows one of two things may happen to them. They may become sexually promiscuous, sleeping around with scores of men as if to confirm their femininity. Or they may be very clumsy around men, shy and unable to relate to them. Boys also need their dads' affirmation to feel secure in their masculinity.

Giving Affection

In addition to provision, attention, and affirmation, a dad also needs to give affection. He can't be emotionally distant, insensitive, or callous. Unfortunately, that seemed to be what men tried to be during the first part of the twentieth century. Traditional fathers focused on authority and power. They were disciplinarians and breadwinners, not nurturers; they left that to the mothers. To yield power, they thought they had to give up their innate tenderness and desire for intimacy. They had to be tough and that did not include being tender.[2] "Fathers with fangs" one expert calls them.

Many baby-boomers grew up with such dads and now want to be different than their fathers were. They aim at being physically affectionate and emotionally expressive, like the man who said, "I try to spend some time every day hugging my kids or touching them or telling them I love them."[3] In creating this image of the "new man," they are both right and wrong. They are right about it being a legitimate picture of a father; they are wrong about it being new. The idea that dads should act tenderly toward their kids is as old as fatherhood itself. More than a century ago, Tocqueville observed, "The relations of father and son becomes more intimate and affectionate; rules and authority are less talked of; confidence and tenderness are oftentimes increased and would it seem that the natural bond is drawn closer."[4]

Think of what must have been Paul's idea of a father when he wrote to the Thessalonian Christians, "For you know that we dealt with each of you as a father deals with his own children, encouraging, comforting and urging you to live lives worthy of God" (1 Thes 2:11).

Abundant research confirms the need for fathers to be affectionate. The massive research project done by the National Center for Fathering makes this very clear. A strong father is involved with his children, playing or working with them, tending to daily routines or just spending unstructured time with them. He is also nurturing; he shows affection and is intimate in spontaneous, not self-conscious, ways.

The degree of a father's active, involved affection toward his children is the most important factor related to the normal heterosexual role development in a child. Research studies have shown that the father who is affectionate and involved with his child is most likely to foster masculinity in his son. Boys are more likely to identify with fathers when they are rewarding and affectionate toward them than if they are not. The finding of one research project is very convincing. A study of boys who had trouble with their sex role as men found that 75 percent of them never had a normal, close relationship with a father or father substitute.[5] Also, normal feminine role development in girls is also related to a warm, nurturant relationship with the mother.[6]

When discussing what our fathers meant to us, one man told of a unique personal gift his father had given him. His dad, a farmer, was always the last one to the dinner table in the evening because he had to wash up after his work. En route to his chair, his father always stopped behind him and placed both of his hands on his son's shoulders while he looked over his family; then he sat down for the meal. This meant so much to this man that all during his boyhood he made sure he got to his seat before his father entered the room so he could feel those big, strong, and warm hands on his shoulders. Through that touch he sensed his dad's protective, affirming, affectionate leadership. That father was a Power Dad. Make sure your family has one. Only you have the power to give your kid a father's touch.

POWER ACTIONS

Get out your "honey-do" list and knock off an item a day or a week until they are done.

Next, make a list of seven things that are great about each of your kids. Affirm your children in those areas, once a day for a week. It may work so well that you'll have to come up with a new seven every week.

"Dad, are we having quality time yet?"

FOUR

RECOGNIZE THE REWARDS

The Payoff Is Unlike Any Other

POWER VERSE

Sons are a heritage from the Lord, children a reward from him. PSALMS 127:3

POWER LESSON

In ancient times, children were an obvious blessing; another child equaled another farmhand. Children were necessary for survival and old-age economic security. The psalmist sang of them as "a heritage from the Lord... a reward from him. Like arrows in the hands of a warrior are sons born in one's youth. Blessed is the man whose quiver is full of them" (Ps 127:3-5). For them, many children made a full quiver; for us, just the thought of a few makes us quiver. Then, children were a fiscal asset. Today, they often seem a fiscal liability. Estimates of what it costs to raise a child today are well into six figures. If children are a blessing, many of us moderns ask, "Just how much blessing can I handle?"

Because raising kids is so costly, some run the risk of devaluing them, of deeming them a nuisance. The prevalence of abortion and child abuse shows that hundreds of thousands of American children seem more of an annoyance than an asset. We often hear more talk of the responsibility of parenting than of the rewards. Dads may do their thing to avoid guilt or feelings of failure. The stick, not the carrot, prods them on. For such parents, Barbara Bush's words strike home:

> As important as your obligation as a doctor, a lawyer or a business leader may be, your human connections with your spouse, your children and your friends are the most important investment you will ever make. At the end of your life, you will never regret not having passed one more test, not winning one more verdict or not closing one more deal; but you will regret time not spent with your spouse, your children or your friends.[1]

The Rewards of Parenting

There seems to be little thought today of the rewards for raising children. The depreciation of children goes hand in hand with the devaluing of the roles of mother and father. Yet, our vocations reward us with prestige and money, pressuring us to go for them even at the expense of family life.

Our quest for other prizes can interfere with being a good parent or even being one at all. For many, the fast track is more appealing than the mommy or daddy track. Better to buy a boat than have another child—the wail of an outboard engine beats the cry of a baby. On Saturday, eighteen holes of golf or eight hours of overtime sound better than three hours of Monopoly. Many couples are choosing not to have kids, believing *it's more blessed to live than to conceive.*

If we are going to be first-class dads, we've got to elevate the role of father, putting it right up there with plumber, doctor—yes, even lawyer. Stressing the responsibility is one way to do that. But thinking about the rewards will also help.

For starters, there's the satisfaction of doing what comes naturally. Ninety percent of the motivation to be a father is embedded deeply in our hearts. Parenting is a response to the instinctive craving to produce and care for the next generation. If we thought too much about it, we might forgo having children. Arguments pile up: too much work and too expensive, the times are too depressing, and we aren't sure if we'll make good parents. So, many of us don't think about it; we just do it.

Most people have a sort of baby hunger. Their creative powers are linked to their reproductive system. Jesus affirmed this human drive to reproduce. "A woman giving birth to a child has pain because her time has come; but when her baby is born she forgets the anguish because of her joy that a child is born into the world" (Jn 16:21).

Sure, there's a sacrifice involved in raising a child, but that's more than compensated by the sheer joy of having one. I asked a friend what were the rewards of being a father. Right away he said, "I just look at my daughter and think, 'She's my kid.'" That satisfaction is not completely explicable; it just is.

How do you explain what you feel when your toddler smiles at you? Or the thrill of hearing your child shriek, "Daddy's home"? What a familiar giggle or sound of a little voice does to a dad is beyond analysis. So, too, the enchantment of watching a tiny son or daughter play peek-a-boo through miniature fingers, or listening to your kid play "Twinkle, Twinkle, Little Star" at the violin recital, or watching your son make his first touchdown.

Some scientists explain that this special attachment we have to our kids is in our genes. This drives us to reproduce and creates in us the satisfaction of doing so. We Christians explain it another way—the fulfillment of being a dad originates with God, who has built within us the desire to reproduce. And when we do we are co-creators with the heavenly Father, following his plan for us. For he has said to us, "Be fruitful and increase in number; fill the earth" (Gn 1:28).

"My Dad takes his role seriously."

Besides all this, there is the joy of knowing a baby is the fruit of your love affair with your wife. It was an expression of your passion that led to your child's conception. When I looked at our newborn children, I had that intense feeling of oneness with Ginger, as I realized each was a combination of the two of us. Being one flesh in marriage, we had actually become one flesh in our children.

If your child is a stepchild or adopted, the feeling will be different; yet caring for a child together is a profound expression of the unity and love you have with your wife.

There are other perks for dads, whether your kids were conceived by you or not. There are many unique things you would probably not do or experience if you were not a father.

You might never get to teach a child to swing a baseball bat or to use a computer. You wouldn't know what it's like to be aroused at 5:00 A.M. by an excited child on Christmas morning. You wouldn't feel the warmth a little hug brings when you tuck a sleepy child in bed. And would your life really be the same without the excuse to read all those Dr. Seuss books or watch Sesame Street programs?

You'd miss watching a child grow. In the early years, it's week by week—the astonishment of seeing them learn words so fast and move from one phase to another.

You'd miss the opportunity to understand your own father and mother better as you relive your own childhood. My own sons, who are now dads themselves, have told me how they know me better because they understand the joys, frustrations, and thoughts I had as their father.

And kids contribute to your own personal growth. Living with them changes you. While it's happening, it may hurt—rather like being stretched on a medieval torture device. Yet, when you look back, you see the stretching was for the better. Though parenting is tough, it toughens. So goes the saying, "I used to think that adults made children; now I know that children make adults." Before you had a child, you probably were not aware how different your life would be—how different you would become. Pushed one way, then pulled another, your life will often be torn apart and you will be forced to put yourself together. The role you play will constantly switch: dad of a toddler, then of a school-age child and teenager, then father of the bride, etc. You will have to reinvent yourself over and over again. At times, it will be excruciatingly difficult. But in the end, if you respond correctly to the process, your own maturity will be one of the greatest rewards of having been a parent.

And then there's the prize of friendship. Once grown, adult children can be among your best friends. If you've invested in them, they will eventually invest in you. If you've loved them, they will love you back. Being with someone you've seen develop from a helpless six-pound fledgling into a mature, competent adult, knowing you played a major part in that development—that is the ultimate payback.

It is the reward that comes from giving. In the end, the satisfaction of fatherhood is not from any contribution your kids make to you, but from what you make to them. It is to experience what Jesus said, "It is more blessed to give than to receive" (Acts 20:35).

POWER ACTIONS

This weekend, set aside the lawn care (or the snow shoveling), the paperwork, the to-do lists, and even the honey-do list. Grab your kids and head to a park. Play a game that all the children can take part in. When you're done, go get ice cream or hot chocolate. Sit around the table and look each one right in the eyes and say, "I love you." It will be the best time you've had in—well—who knows how long?

FIVE

FACE YOUR FEAR

Beware the Paranoid Parent Syndrome

POWER VERSE

Do not be anxious about anything, but in everything, by prayer and petition, with thanksgiving, present your requests to God. And the peace of God, which transcends all understanding, will guard your hearts and your minds in Christ Jesus. PHILIPPIANS 4:6

POWER LESSON

When my family and I were in the Philippines as missionaries, my wife, Ginger, and I came down with a severe case of anxiety. In the Christian school our children attended, bad news broke out: a number of teens were caught doing drugs. At first, only a few of the kids were named and the teachers weren't sure how widespread the practice was. As a result, emotional tremors spread through hundreds of parents. Questions were asked, and trust between parents and children was tested. What shook us was the fact that one of the identified drug users was our son's best friend. Though teachers assured us that our son was not among the guilty students, we remained frightened.

During this time, one afternoon our son didn't arrive home when the school bus did. Our daughter Becky told us he had gotten out midway during the hour-long drive home. What would make him get off the bus in the middle of metropolitan Manila? Our dread mixed with doubt and anger, which only made us think the worst; and when he finally did come home, we overreacted. We turned his misdemeanor into a felony, showing little trust and turning into the likes of medieval inquisitioners. We both fried and grilled him, but he coughed up no answers; we were left to guess where he had been and why. For weeks afterward I was Sherlock Holmes and my wife Miss Marple, as we watched him like private eyes. We were afraid that he was in big trouble and sure that we were failures. His only explanation was that he felt like getting off the bus and going to the shopping center.

For fifteen years I felt bad about this overreaction and wondered about the mystery. So I asked Chuck, now grown, to tell us what he had been up to. Remember when you got off the bus early? Why? Was it drugs? A girl, maybe? "No, Dad, I just felt like it. Perhaps I was trying to be a little independent." I laughed when he told me and wished I had had a better sense of humor then and less fear and mistrust.

Anxiety-Free Fathering

Fear can force fathers to fantasize wildly about what their children are up to, pushing them to be ultrasuspicious, overstrict, and overprotective at the least sign of strangeness.

The Bible suggests that we do nothing based on anxiety. Paul wrote, "Do not be anxious about anything" (Phil 4:6). This doesn't mean we shouldn't be concerned. In fact, Paul conceded that he was deeply concerned for all the churches (see 2 Corinthians 11:28). Some intelligent caution can keep us on the alert. We shouldn't face life glibly. But there is a point where legitimate concern turns into plain old senseless worry. God warns against it because it shows a lack of faith in his ability to care for us. Extreme worry can destroy us internally and cause us to do destructive things to our kids.

There are ways to avoid this. First, Paul says to pray—and do it "in everything" (Phil 4:6). As one Bible teacher put it, "Pray about nothing and you'll worry about everything; pray about everything and you'll worry about nothing."

Not only can we pray about things we might be anxious about, but we can pray about our anxiety. This is essentially what the apostle Peter meant when he said, "Cast all your anxiety on him because he cares for you" (1 Pt 5:7). The picture here is of someone throwing a pack onto a horse so that he won't have to carry the load any longer. As parents, we must believe what Peter says, that God cares for us. It is faith, not fear, that makes us power dads. Above all we must trust God for our children.

Paul says to pray with thanksgiving. We should wrap up our petitions with a positive attitude of gratitude. Worry, like fog disappearing in the rising sun, dissipates in the warm glow of gratitude. When worried, try telling God about all the good things that have happened or are happening to you. It's hard to be terribly anxious and grateful at the same time.

Also, we need to trust our kids more. When a teenager starts to flap his wings in his parents' faces, the parents sometimes get harsher and stricter than they've ever been, believing that they have failed up to that point and now must make this child turn out right. Instead, they need to realize that they have had input and influence for thirteen or more years; now they need to rely on their past training.

My wife and I were determined to never surrender to panic or despair on account of our children. When we had a few extremely tense years with a son, I clutched tightly a verse of Scripture I had found, "Weeping may remain for a night, but rejoicing comes in the morning" (Ps 30:5). I took this verse as an assertion of hope for those who trust in God, and so I prayed and hoped. Months later, I shared with Ginger how this promise had heartened me. To my surprise, she confided that she had been resting in this same verse. Our weeping did give way to rejoicing as our dark night with our son turned into a splendid morning. When our children wander in murky, gloomy paths, it's important that we continue to believe there is light ahead.

Besides fear, we fathers have to deal with failure. Some people who try to encourage parents end up scaring them. They use Proverbs 22:6 to do it. "See," they say, "if you raise a child right, he will do right." The implication is that if he doesn't do right, you've done wrong. Intending to pat us on the head to encourage us, they end up clubbing us, filling us with anxiety and guilt.

Once I asked a man about his children. During the long pause before he answered, his head drooped and his eyes shifted back and forth as if he were absentmindedly looking for something he'd lost. He looked beaten, defeated. He told me about his son, who lives in another state and is an alcoholic. His wife had a nervous breakdown. Eventually, because of these problems he resigned from his job as a minister. Like many Christian parents, he and his wife apparently blamed themselves for their son's problem. When I asked this former minister if he believed parents can always make their kids turn out right, he didn't answer. He just turned away. Remorse had apparently taken the edge off his life. Like many he believed that with the kids gone wrong, nothing would be right again.

We must be careful not to allow our children to tear our house down around us. If they choose a destructive path, we must do what we can to help, but we must not wallow in self-condemnation that destroys whatever we have left.

This applies to those who have failed and are now oppressed by guilt, and to those who are so afraid to fail they are terrorized by anxiety. These feelings hinder fathers just as they do athletes. Pitchers and quarterbacks have to loosen up. They can't play their best if they are petrified by the fear of losing. Fathers also need to be a bit loose; by making everything the proverbial "federal case," they turn the home into a pressure cooker. My family knows what this is like because I was so obsessed about being a good father that I had difficulty relaxing. Often my wife said to me, "Take it easy; enjoy the kids."

We should especially avoid letting some feeling of failure turn us into bad fathers, especially when our children become teens and they begin to act strangely. Their behavior sometimes defies explanation, and they enjoy making us second guess and wonder about them. What we judge to be mystery, they consider privacy. They don't always want us to know what's going on; this is part of their growing up and out.

A thirteen-year-old boy wants a cassette player. His parents say, "Not now; the money's not there for it." Two days later he comes home with one; when asked where he got it, he says he traded something for it or refuses to say. Or a fourteen-year-old daughter comes to her mother sobbing, saying that she just ripped a button off the blouse she was going to wear. Her mother says, "Oh, I'm sorry; I'll sew it on for you." The daughter turns away, slamming the door, saying, "You don't really care."[1] Any little deviation from normalcy will send some parents into panicville. Most of this panic is due to the parents' deep dread of failure. Of the fourteen worries listed in one survey of parents, none drew as high a rating as the worry over "the job I am doing in raising this child."[2]

We have to keep on doing our best with confidence. Even if

we have blundered, we have to stay on the job, alert and wise. Like the running back who has to stay in the game after fumbling the ball, we need to recover and go forward. Referring to this, the late Dave Simmons, once a pro football player, always gave this advice to the fathers in his seminars, "Play one play at a time." Stay in there. Don't freeze. Keep loose. Make your next play.

POWER ACTIONS

Maybe you've dropped the ball. If you've been a dad for any length of time, you've probably lost your temper when you should have stayed calm, or you didn't make it to an important family activity because of work. If family life is like a ball game, then we've all dropped the ball a few times. What can you do now? Play the next play. Some night this week, play a game with your kids—baseball, basketball, video, or board game. When it's over, let your kids know that there are times that you felt like you failed, dropped the ball, or landed on the wrong square. Let them know you're sorry. Then tell them that there is another play. The game isn't over. You'll do your best. You may drop the ball again, but together as a family you'll win the game.

SIX

BE CONSISTENT

Be It Again, Dad

POWER VERSE

A man of understanding is even-tempered.   PROVERBS 17:27

POWER LESSON

One researcher found that kids feel more comfortable approaching mom with their requests and problems than dad. The reason: they are never quite sure how he'll react. Sometimes he's helpful; at other times he's just plain harsh. It depends on his mood. No wonder that a major trait of strong fathers is consistency.[1]

A consistent father has two major qualities. *Predictability* is the first. Family members don't have to guess what dad might say or do in a given situation. His emotions and moods aren't always shifting: "A man of understanding is even-tempered" (Prv 17:27). The second quality is *integrity*. There is a harmony between what a father is on the inside and how he lives on the outside. Thus, he isn't hypocritical. His walk and talk closely match.

Imagine what it's like for a child to live with an ever-changing father. On Thursday, the two-year-old climbs onto his smiling father's lap to receive warm hugs. On Friday, the same two-year-old crawls onto his drunken father's lap and gets pushed aside and sworn at. At this early age, the child is not able to understand the cause of this Dr. Jekyll and Mr. Hyde behavior. Unable to process it and blame her father, she takes upon herself the brunt of his inconsistent behavior.

And the damage to her is considerable. For one thing, it thwarts her ability to trust. She will be shyly afraid of people or bitterly distrustful, and she will react to other men as she did her father. Some grown women are like timid puppies around men. I've met a few who were so badly abused that they would actually flinch if you got within a normal distance of them.

An unpredictable father will also prevent a child from learning to master his environment, which is one of his major life tasks. At different points in a child's development, his mastery will be demonstrated in a variety of ways, from striving for good school grades to developing a fierce competitive spirit as seen at high school and college sports events. Children who live in families where a behavior is rewarded one time and punished the next have trouble relying on themselves to control their lives. Instead, they depend on others. They do this by getting cues from their environment. They are not taught to follow their feelings but rather to follow the actions of another—to *react* rather than *act*. They have trouble learning which action is the right one, because their parents' reaction to what they do keeps changing. This means that what is right or wrong keeps changing. The perceptive child learns how to watch the family, so that under each changing set of circumstances he will know how to act. When the cues keep changing and the consequences for mistakes are severe, the child becomes dependent on these external cues to know what to do. The brighter the child, the more in tune with his environment he will be, and the more anxious he will become. He will know that he is not behaving as expected, and will be more confused until he learns the dysfunctional family rule of not depending on himself but rather on the cues around him.

By learning to trust only external cues, such children also learn that feeling good can come only from a source outside of themselves. This helps explain why many children of alcoholics learn to depend on others and not themselves in a relationship. This is also why many children from addictive families learn to pursue external rewards—to eat, shop, drink, do drugs, work, gamble, spend, or have sex compulsively.[2]

Besides unpredictability, the other aspect of inconsistency—being hypocritical—damages children. It also confuses them about right and wrong, since they aren't sure whether to find it in dad's words or his actions. This makes it hard for them to be dedicated Christians. In my experience, nothing thwarts children's faith in God like a parent's failure to back their beliefs with actions.

Striving for Consistency

Even though you won't be perfectly consistent with your children, you should strive for this. And there are ways to do it.

1. Examine yourself to see if there is an underlying reason for your inconsistency. Any personal addiction or compulsion could be a major cause of fluctuating moods and behavior. It might be alcohol or prescription drugs. Even a fixation on food or achievement can make you unpredictable. So-called workaholics are constantly in need of a "success fix" to make them feel good. In between they are driven, sullen, and depressed. Their kids aren't always sure if dad will be up or down, if he will keep his promise to play with them or break it because he's too busy.

Some of us are just plain moody. Our bouts with anger or depression make us unpredictable. Our kids "walk on eggs," hoping not to set us off, wondering whether we are approachable or not. Indecision also can make some of us unpredictable. When we have a hard time dealing with problems or making decisions, we don't like it when our kids bring their requests or problems to us. We react impulsively and angrily, signaling a "don't bother me" attitude. After thinking it over, we may act sensibly.

Figure yourself out and try to work on what makes you inconsistent. Until you do that, you won't be consistent.

2. *Work on being more emotionally stable.* Feelings are a major cause of a father's unpredictability. This may be demonstrated by the fact that incidents of child abuse rise and fall with the fluctuation in unemployment figures. Men out of work often become men out of control because they are depressed and distressed by their unemployment. The more you work on understanding and dealing with your emotions, the better you will deal with your children.

3. *To reduce the impact of inconsistency on children, apologize to them when you act this way.* Not understanding why you aren't always the same is what is most troubling to children. They feel confused and guilty, blaming themselves for making you react the way you do. They aren't wise enough to figure out that the problem was not what they said or did, but what you were feeling. If you ask for forgiveness and explain why you acted as you did, you will help them immensely. If you say, "I was in an angry mood," or, "I have this problem of reacting too quickly," it will go a long way toward helping them make sense of the situation.

4. *Try hard to keep promises.* Five centuries before Christ a rabbi said, "Never promise something to a child and not give it to him, because in that way he learns to lie."[3] Fathers often believe it is more acceptable to break a promise to a family

member than to someone else. We believe a wife and child will be more understanding and flexible than a boss, a church member, or a friend. Therefore, we postpone the family picnic or trip to Six Flags to attend a hastily called meeting of a board or committee. However, the message we send to the family is that they are not as important as these other commitments and that Dad can't be relied on. Imagine how doing the opposite on occasion would make your child feel—if she knew you said "no" to something important because you had promised to take her to a movie or to the library.

Strive for consistency in all areas of your family life. Research shows that an effective father is consistent, not only in his mood swings, but in his presence in the family, in his daily schedule, and in his hobbies and interests.[4] Think about what it means to a kid to know his father's daily and weekly schedule and be assured he has a place in it. You like to look forward to good times: eighteen holes on a Saturday morning with some guys, a romantic evening with your wife, etc. If your kid doesn't know whether or not you'll be around or when, he is deprived of looking forward to good times with you. If he knows you'll be home at a regular hour or that he'll have time with you each Saturday afternoon, it provides stability in his life.

There's profit in having steadiness in the hobbies and recreational activities you share with your kids. Perhaps it's playing musical instruments together, building model planes, fishing, or stamp or coin collecting. These activities give your children something by which they can define their family.[5]

For so many of today's children, life is chaotic and uncertain. They go to school in the morning not sure their mothers and fathers will still be living together when they get home, or whether their parents will be delightful or dismal. Home, the place meant to provide them some security, has become as unsure as the world around them. Blessed are those kids who have a dad they can count on.

POWER ACTIONS

Think back to your childhood. What was one thing that you really enjoyed doing in your spare time? Did you build model airplanes? Cars? Boats? Maybe it was a collection of coins or stamps? Pick out one of your favorite things and do it with your children to bring them into your life. You won't believe how much they'll enjoy discovering who Dad was as a kid. Once the project is set, you will need to set a schedule. If your work hours change from week to week, make it clear each week when your hobby night or day will be. Your kids will learn to trust you and you'll have a great time together.

"You know, son, being a daddy is like watching a Disney movie. The more you see me, the more you want to see me. I like that."

SEVEN

DEAL WITH YOUR PAST

To Be a Dad, First Be a Son

POWER VERSE
I, the Lord your God, am a jealous God, punishing the children for the sin of the fathers to the third and fourth generation of those who hate me, but showing love to thousands who love me and keep my commandments.   EXODUS 20:4

POWER LESSON
   This verse contains the frightening thought that kids will be punished for the sins of the fathers. Yet, it doesn't mean these children are blameless, because they also hate God just as their parents did. And the passage is really quite positive: God will show love to countless generations that love and obey him. The point of the passage is that generations influence one another for good or for ill. We impact our children's lives just as our parents did ours.
   Dave Simmons' life is a somber example of this. His father, Amos, was a problem drinker who was extremely demanding. He rarely said a kind word to Dave, always prodding him with harsh criticism to do better, bracing his orders with beatings and verbal assaults.
   When Dave played football in high school, his father was unrelenting in his criticisms. In the backyard of his home, after every game his dad would point out Dave's errors. "Most boys

got butterflies in the stomach before the game; I got them afterwards," Dave recalls. "Facing my father was more stressful than facing any opposing team." By the time he entered college he hated his father. He chose to attend the University of Georgia simply because it was further away from Amos than any other school that offered him a scholarship.

After college, hearing he had just become the second round draft pick of the St. Louis Cardinal's professional football club, he telephoned his father to share the news. Amos responded, "How does it feel to be second?"

Despite the hateful feelings he had for his father, Dave Simmons began to build a bridge to his dad. Christ had come into his life during the college years, and it was God's love that made him turn to his father. In their conversations, Dave learned what Amos' father had been like. A tough lumberjack, he was known for his quick temper, once destroying a pickup truck with a sledgehammer because it wouldn't start. Amos had been beaten by his dad.

"By the time my father died, we had become friends," Dave said. When he married and had children, he believed the negative influence of his father was settled, but he was shocked to find out it wasn't. It was after attending a simple elementary school basketball game that he became aware of the extent of his father's impact upon him. David, his wife, and daughter went to this game to see their son play in his first athletic event. Brandon played rather badly; on their way home, David proceeded to tell him so. He critically scoured the small boy sitting beside him in the car, pointing out all the mistakes he had made during the game. Arriving home in tears, Brandon rushed into the house, followed by David's wife and daughter who had been seated in the backseat. When he arrived at the front door, Dave found his wife was waiting for him. Angrily, she blustered, "David! You are just like your father!" No jolt on the football field hit any harder than those words. How could he begin to do to his own son what he had so despised his father for doing to him?

The answer is that we are more like our fathers than some of us care to admit. And it is crucial for us to recognize this, particularly if our fathers didn't do their job well.

Protecting the Past

Despite all the talk about dysfunctional families, many men are unwilling to admit their parents may have failed them. One reason for this is that they don't realize there are two types of abuse: passive and active. People who were passively abused were simply neglected. Such people think that because their parents didn't scream at them, beat them, or otherwise actively abuse them, they were not mistreated. But neglect can be a severe form of abuse. According to the Bible, children need to be loved, taught, disciplined, encouraged, and cared for. If you failed to get these in sufficient supply, you were no doubt hurt in some way.

Even those who came from physically abusive homes may not realize how bad they were, simply because they never learned what a normal home was like. Somehow it never occurred to them that it was abnormal to watch your drunken father stumble up the porch steps headlong into a screaming battle with your mother. Or that it was unusual to cringe in your bedroom listening to an angry father's footsteps, praying he wouldn't stop at your room to pick a fight. People who grew up in such families often think they were quite average. Unless their parents admitted their problem and got help, they never thought things were out of line.

Still another reason to overlook parents' faults is that troubled families teach us to do so. Dysfunctional families are permeated with denial. Even the most severe mistreatment is not seen for what it is. "It's OK, kids," a battered wife might say. "Daddy only broke my arm this time." As a result, people who spring from these homes think things were OK. Even as adults, sexually abused children have a hard time admitting that what happened was wrong, covering up with, "Dad was only trying to teach me about sex." "It really wasn't so bad." They tell themselves this because that's what they were told.

A sense of loyalty also plays a part in seeing our parents' shortcomings. When we were children we wanted to protect them; we needed them and were told we should love them. Acknowledging that they failed us or deliberately abused us makes us feel bad, even guilty. We feel that we are betraying them.

Troubled families still have their joyful moments just as good families have bad ones. Usually the worst of parents do some things right some of the time.

Of course, many of us who dismiss any personal problems stemming from our troubled childhood families do it because we believe we've left them all behind. Becoming adults, we simply outgrew them.

Yet, research suggests that our childhood experiences have a powerful impact on us as adults. Some persons barely escape. In the case of incest victims, research shows that only 23 percent of the victims survive without any adverse effects.[1]

A summary of ten other research projects describes the following traits common to kids from alcoholic homes: poor self-concept, low frustration tolerance, poor academic performance, higher incidence of depression, hyperactivity, emotional and behavioral disorders, sexual confusion, and a variety of physical complaints.[2] One of the most convincing pieces of research was a study on the long-term effects of an act of violence. The project focused on adults who, though not physically abused themselves, watched one parent strike the other. Testing showed they were clearly more anxious than those who came from homes where there was a more satisfying marital relationship. Also, the women in the study who viewed marital violence were more aggressive and depressed than other women.[3]

Some of us tune out the past because we don't want to admit we may be less than perfect or in need of help. After all, we survived. Our childhood may have made us strong and independent. We think of ourselves as super-strong. It's not easy for us to admit we hurt.

Some people actually block out the past, burying the memories and feelings like campers bury their garbage. Incest survivors have vague persistent feelings that something happened, but no memories. I know of men who can't remember a thing that happened during the first ten or fifteen years of their lives.

Breaking the Cycle

There is yet another reason why you might be prone to overlook any negative influence your father or mother had on you. Christians tend to think that such influence was dealt with when they were born again. A favorite verse in the King James Version assures us: "If any man be in Christ, he is a new creature... behold, all things are become new" (2 Cor 5:17, KJV). Transfixed on the future we say with the apostle Paul, "Forgetting what is behind... I press on toward the goal to win the prize for which God has called me heavenward in Christ Jesus" (Phil 3:13-14). Like the butterfly out of the cocoon, we can soar into the future, unhindered by our yesterdays.

We need to realize that Christ does change us when we first meet him, but he doesn't make us perfect. The King James translation of 2 Corinthians 5:17 is inadequate. It is not, "Behold, all things are become new," but, "Behold, new things have come." Potentially, on the cross, the old things have passed away. In him there is power for a moral life, a loving life. But the new will not come without doing combat with the old. We still have natures that are capable of sin, and those sinful natures, with their weaknesses and tendencies to do wrong, have been shaped by the past. This explains why we each deal with different issues. The old natures of some persons are easily angered. Other Christians rarely get fighting mad, but may grapple with pride, lust, or greed. One man said to me, "I control more temper in a day than some Christians do in a lifetime." We each face varying temptations and bear different burdens.

The most alarming thing about families is that they seem to produce in kind. Dysfunctional families produce dysfunctional families. There is a powerful cycle at work. It is not that every adult child of an alcoholic home becomes an alcoholic. But it's likely that the one who comes from such a home will have some traits that threaten the welfare of his marriage and family.

To break that cycle, you must admit that you were negatively impacted. To do so is not a betrayal of your family. Nor is doing so a way of blaming your parents. Rather, it is a way of explaining yourself.

Perhaps you are more like your father than you thought. Maybe you have a personal problem grounded in your past, that hinders you from being a good father.

To be an effective dad, you need to be an honest one, one who appraises his weaknesses and strengths and then seeks to improve. "The wisdom of the prudent is to give thought to their ways, but the folly of fools is deception" (Prv 14:8). A good way to view yourself objectively is to answer the question, "How much am I like my father and mother?" Be sure to list their strengths as well as weaknesses. Like family heirlooms, we pass traits down to the next generation. Some of these we are better off without. Find out what they are.

POWER ACTIONS

List all of the emotions you think your father had. Now list his behaviors. After making these two lists, evaluate yourself in the light of them. Next, list both his strengths and weaknesses. Now compare yourself with your lists. Where have you imitated and where have you just followed his lead? What needs to be changed? Take one area from the list that needs change and work on it until your actions match up to your new thinking. Pick one that you can win at. It will make the next one and the one after that easier to attempt.

"Who would need something like that?"

EIGHT

TAP INTO THE POWER SOURCE

When You're Weak, You're Strong

POWER VERSE

His divine power has given us everything we need for life and godliness through our knowledge of him who called us.

2 Peter 1:3

POWER LESSON

Norbert Wiener has influenced modern life even more than computer whiz Bill Gates. Wiener is the brains behind the modern computer and one of the true geniuses of all times. Yet, this is what he wrote about being a father: "I am neither certain of the correctness of the policies I have adopted nor ashamed. One has only one life to live and there is not enough time to master the art of being a parent."[1]

Very intelligent men have trouble being fathers. I'm told that some CEOs of major companies drive around the block several times just to summon up courage to enter their homes. They can manage large companies, but can't handle their teenage sons. In their companies they feel powerful; in their homes, powerless. This is true partly because our society does not support parent power. Our kids aren't taught as they once were by schools, churches, and law enforcement agencies to obey their parents.

Another reason men feel powerless at home is that it takes a different set of tools to be an executive than it does to be a father. The corporation puts power into the executive's hands. As a boss, a man can sack a defiant subordinate, but a father can't fire his son. The boss has studied long and hard to learn the skills of an executive, but his schooling for being a parent has been minimal. What's true of these front office guys is just as true for other men. We've been trained to be mechanics, lawyers, plumbers, teachers, and the like, but not to be dads. The result is that many men feel helpless as fathers.

Fathers have been powerless in their homes for many years. Historians tell us that in the early 1800s mothers took over the nurturing of children when, at the beginning of the industrial revolution, men's work took them outside the home. As a result, dads began to feel out of place.

Before the 1800s, a father was not only present in the home but was a central figure. Unlike today, in child custody disputes the courts always awarded the children to the fathers. In those days when adult children wrote home, they addressed their letters to Dad, somewhere inserting a casual, "Say hello to Mother."[2] Perhaps this evidence suggests fathers unfairly dominated home life, which is certainly not the ideal. But it proves that American men of the past were often heavily involved in family life.

Today too few dads are in the family picture, and we are recognizing the cost of their absence. More problems come out of homes of single mothers than from two-parent homes. Without dads, kids tend to do poorly in school, are more prone toward drugs, have more emotional disorders, and are more likely to be delinquent. Having a man around the house is not the full answer to the problems kids have, but it makes a big difference. To be around, a father has *to be around*. Too many men are present physically but virtually absent, because they are uninvolved in the life of their families.

Men need to recover Father Power and to exert it for good. By power, we're not talking about domination, but influence—being a leader, not a boss. Most women I know would welcome some help in running the family. They are less afraid of a husband taking charge than they are that he won't.

What Is a Power Dad?

A Power Dad is one who gets off the bench and enters the family arena in order to make a difference—through his dedication, his example, his guidance, his teaching, and his love. Fathers have many avenues of power to influence the next generation. The purpose of this book is to describe those avenues to you and to help you put them into practice. To do so will require effort—and faith.

A dad's power comes from the heavenly Father's power. The Bible often speaks of this power, and Paul prayed for Christians to have it: "I pray also... that you may know... his incomparably great power for us who believe. That power is like the working of his mighty strength, which he exerted in Christ when he raised him from the dead" (Eph 1:18-20).

You may have heard it said, "Pray as if it all depended on God, and work as if it all depended on you." There is some truth to this, but as Christians we must pray and work, always knowing it all depends on God. Power results from trusting God—while we do our best. Christians know their best is not enough and recognize their inadequacy without God. This is why the apostle Paul could make the seemingly absurd statement, "When I am weak, then I am strong" (2 Cor 12:10). Paul believed that God's power was most displayed in him whenever he was helpless.

Tapping into God's Power

This was David's attitude when he faced the giant Goliath. Going up against that monstrous warrior, he refused to accept the armor and sword King Saul offered him and chose a slingshot instead. It took faith to believe that he could beat the giant with only a slingshot, but it would have taken a lot more faith to stumble onto the battlefield in armor he had never before used. He refused them because he had never practiced in them, and he went to face Goliath with his best weapons—his faith and a sling.

When he confronted the blustering, swaggering Goliath, he didn't brag, "I've come to you in the name of the Davidic Slingshot Society." Rather, he declared, "I come against you in the name of the Lord Almighty.... This day the Lord will hand you over to me, and I'll strike you down.... For the battle is the Lord's" (1 Sm 17:45-47).

David knew that winning his battle required more than his slingshot expertise. It required faith in God, and that made him a courageous and confident man.

Paul, too, recognized this need: "Stand firm in the faith; be men of courage; be strong" (1 Cor 16:13).

As dads, we most of all need faith. Being a father is an awesome task, and few of us feel ready for it. Could it be that our lack of faith is the reason so many of us don't even try to father? Or if we do, we give up trying too soon? God promises us power and also the ability to be men of love, joy, peace, patience, kindness, goodness, faithfulness, gentleness, and self-control (see Galatians 5:22-23). There is no better list of the traits of an effective father than this.

These nine traits of the Spirit are called the "fruit of the Spirit," meaning the Holy Spirit produces them in us. To tap into God's power we must learn to be in touch with him.

When we do, we are "filled with the Spirit" (Eph 5:18). Paul says it is somewhat similar to being drunk with wine. By that he means that just as a person is controlled by the alcohol he has taken into his system, so a Christian is controlled by the Holy Spirit he has taken into his heart. Paul doesn't mean that we will do odd things, as some Christians seem to think. There is nothing weird about what the Holy Spirit produces: love, patience, self-control, and the like.

To be empowered by the Spirit, there are a number of things we must do.

1. We must surrender to God. The apostle Paul said we should offer our bodies as living sacrifices (see Romans 12:1). This refers to a once-for-all commitment to God. Yet, even after this initial surrender, we will still have to continue to surrender moment by moment in daily matters. When we fail to do so, we thwart the Holy Spirit's work in our lives. The Bible says, "Do not put out the Spirit's fire" (1 Thes 5:19).

2. Keep in touch with God, constantly. This doesn't require your never sinning. It demands we confess any sin we commit. Sin separates us from fellowship with God, and confession restores fellowship.

Sometimes when we lose fellowship with God, we feel the pain of being out of touch with him. Other times we don't feel much of anything. We should not depend on our emotions to tell us whether we are in or out of fellowship. We have to take our relationship with God by faith. If we have surrendered to God and have no unconfessed sin in our lives, we can assume he is with us.

3. Depend on him. This dependence is called being led by the Spirit or living by the Spirit (see Galatians 5:16, 18). It is in contrast to living by our own strength. Our dependence is an awareness that we are not competent in ourselves, but that our competence comes from God (see 2 Corinthians 3:5).

Your dependence or trust will make a major difference in how you perform as a father and even how you read this book. *Power Dads* gives knowledge and techniques for being a good father. You can easily get frustrated and discouraged while trying to practice what this book suggests. Trusting God, not yourself, is the best way to prevent that from happening and give you confidence that you can become a better father.

Walter's Story

Believing you can do something is crucial to success. A man named Walter Davis learned this. Afflicted with polio as a child, he was unable to walk, and doctors said he never would again. But his mother didn't believe them. She tirelessly bathed his legs in warm water and massaged them until Walter was able to walk and eventually to run.

One day while watching a high school track meet, he said to himself, "I am going to become a world champion high jumper," and he set out to reach his goal. With his weak legs objecting, he began to practice. Long hours of practice caused intense pain, but that didn't thwart him.

He married, and during his college days he would talk to his wife about the awful intensity of effort required to succeed on the track field. He shared with her his doubts about whether he could ever reach his goal. Together, they decided he could succeed if only he believed he could. They called their idea "the strength of belief."

The day came when this determined athlete was near his goal. In an indoor track meet, he had just cleared the bar at six feet, eleven and one-half inches. When it was raised another eighth of an inch, the crowd hushed, knowing that if Walter cleared the bar, he would set a new world record. He ran and jumped, but the bar fell with him. He tried again, and again the bar came down. As he faced his third and final try, he remembered the phrase he and his wife had coined—"the strength of belief." He pictured himself clearing the bar. Then he took a deep breath, ran for all he was worth and leaped into the air. And the boy they said would never walk became the world champion high jumper.[3]

Walter Davis believed in himself. It's important to believe in yourself, but it is even more important to believe in God. Believing in God can give you the confidence you need to become the kind of father you want to be. The "strength of belief" can turn you into a world class dad and a champion to your family. God's power can make you a Power Dad.

One final suggestion for tapping into God's power: join a group of closely-knit Christian men.

Because they were alarmed over the number of Christian ministers who were caught in adulterous situations, Howard Hendricks and Chuck Swindoll did a study to find out the reason. Only one thing seemed to be common to most of these pastors: at the time of their infidelity they were not in any deep supporting relationships with other Christians. They found what so many other Christians are discovering today: no one can be a Christian alone.

The New Testament tells us the church should be a support group. We should meet together to spur one another to love and good works. Yet, many of us don't have this kind of backing; our relationships are too few and too superficial. We are free to consult one another about business and technical things, but are often afraid to talk about our personal problems.

We feel free to ask a friend how to plaster a hole in our ceiling, but not how to fill a hole in our soul. In some matters, we don't like to ask for help. It makes us feel weak and exposed.

Women often laugh about (or are frustrated by) the fact that when men drivers are lost, they despise stopping to ask for help. The reason Moses wandered in the wilderness for forty years, someone joked, is that he wouldn't stop to ask for directions.

Something else you receive from being in a group is increased understanding of your problem. As you listen to other men talk about problems similar to yours, you gain insight into your own thoughts, behaviors, and feelings. You will benefit by listening to men who are further along in their growth and parenting skills than you are.

Sharing with others generates hope that you can endure a trial or a problem. As you hear other men tell of their victories, you'll be more confident that you too can succeed.

"Mom says that if I eat all my vegetables, I'll grow up big and strong like Dad."

Men report that being in a close-knit group of men frees them to communicate more intimately with others. Their communicating skills get better, and they feel more at ease talking to their wives and children.

The idea that Christians need each other is not new. In the last century George Whitefield, the great evangelist and friend of John and Charles Wesley, knew this. He advised:

> My brethren,... let us plainly and freely tell one another what God has done for our souls. To this end you would do well, as others have done, to form yourselves into little companies of four or five each, and meet once a week to tell each other what is in your hearts; that you may pray for and comfort one another as need may require.... None, I think, that truly loves his own soul and his brethren as himself, will be shy of opening his heart in order to have their advice, reproof, admonition and prayer, as occasions require. A sincere person will esteem it one of the greatest blessings. None but they who have experienced it can tell the unspeakable advantage of such union and communion of souls.[4]

Whitefield discovered the rewards of being with a group of honest, transparent, accepting Christians. I hope you will too.

POWER ACTIONS

There are many ways to find the spiritual support you need to be an effective father. Make a list of things you need to do to regularly plug into God's power.

ABLE MAN

PART TWO

*Here's to my Dad, who is absolutely tops in my book.
A dad who is loving, caring, giving...*

NINE

BE ALWAYS CHANGING

Make the Long Trip from Head to Habit

POWER VERSE

And we, who with unveiled faces all reflect [or contemplate] the Lord's glory, are being transformed into his likeness with ever-increasing glory, which comes from the Lord, who is the Spirit. 2 CORINTHIANS 3:18

POWER LESSON

"When my teenage daughter asks, 'Dad, may I go out tonight?' I put my education to work," the superintendent of our local high school told me. "First, I sift through all the adolescent psychology courses I've had, then the secondary education classes. Finally, my mind runs through the management courses of my Ph.D. program. Then I confidently reply, 'Go ask your mother.'"

It is difficult to transfer knowledge from the front lobes of our brains to behind the front doors of our homes. Knowledge is not enough. It takes something more to change us. Most fathers and mothers could write a list of what it takes to be a good parent. Yet, writing the list is a long way from living it.

We Christians sometimes kid ourselves into thinking that

simply learning more about the Bible will automatically lead to change. In the early years of my Christian life, I so often thought I had conquered a problem when I hadn't. After hearing a sermon on how to deal with anxiety, I left the church thinking my worrying days were over. I soon learned that wasn't true. Knowing didn't equal growing.

From Head to Habits

1. We have to be constantly aware of our need to apply what we know. When facing a problem, we need to ask ourselves, "What do I already know that will help me deal with this situation?"

A former sailor explained how the Navy taught him to ask this question. In his basic training, he was taught by lecture and films how to handle himself in an emergency. Following weeks of instruction, he and his classmates were taken to a lake where they boarded a strange-looking vessel. They found themselves in a small cabin on the lower deck awaiting further orders. Chatting and drinking Cokes, they were alarmed when the door flew open and a torrent of water came crashing down the stairs. Unable to get out, they stood helplessly waiting for someone to rescue them. When waist high, the water stopped; then it slowly receded. They were spared from drowning, but not from a dressing-down, which came shortly afterward.

An irate officer told them they had flunked the test. The room contained all they needed to close the door and block the water. In this simulated emergency, they had failed to act as they had been taught. Sure, they had passed a written test on the matter, but not the life test.[1]

2. To change we need to be persistent. We are all an assortment of dispositions: tendencies toward thoughts, attitudes, or behavior. We've practiced them so long that they have become a part of us. Some are good, others bad. We have a tendency to be angry, or impatient, or critical. A disposition doesn't change quickly. However, when we force ourselves by God's power to change our behavior for a certain period of time, our disposition will eventually change. We won't feel the urge to get as angry or impatient as we once did. It helps to focus on some area of change for a few months, knowing that eventually it will become easier.

3. Focus on positive action. Concentrate on doing what you should do instead of what you shouldn't. This principle works in improving your golf or tennis game. You concentrate on keeping your wrist straight rather than on not bending it. The idea behind this is that if you consciously think of what you shouldn't do, your mind will play tricks on you and unconsciously you will do it. It's like the guy who told his friend, "Whatever you do, don't think about a white bear." The poor guy was driven to distraction. The more he tried to stop thinking about the beast, the more difficult it became to extract it from his mind.

Of course, this doesn't mean we should never think about what we should not do, since Scripture often lists negatives, such as the Ten Commandments. But it's practically helpful to stress the positive. Thus, the apostle Paul, when explaining how Christians should act, used the metaphor of dressing. We should take off our old clothes of anger, slander, greed, and put on new ones of compassion, love, kindness, patience.

So keep asking yourself, "What new thing should I be putting on when taking off the old?" For example, if you habitually blow your stack when your kid does a certain thing, you should concentrate on being patient or more understanding. So you think, "Be patient," rather than, "Don't be angry." If you are prone to criticize your wife, try harder to say nice things about her. If you are tempted to fantasize about sex with other women, instead of trying not to do so, try fantasizing about your wife or about something else. Otherwise, your efforts to concentrate on not thinking sexually about other women will only tempt you to think about them. This principle of focusing on the positive is also important in disciplining your children, which I'll explain in a later chapter.

4. *To get from precept to practice, constantly remind yourself of the changes you need to make.* After attending a weekend marriage seminar, a man said to me, "This was great, but I think I need it once a month." We too easily forget. By constantly reading and memorizing Scripture, we can inject it into our heart (our inner being) so that it becomes a part of us. Poring over God's truth is like storing food in a cellar. Not only is it available when we need it, but like apples in a storehouse, its odor can permeate the interior of our souls. A person may not even be conscious of how Scripture about anger may be mellowing his bad temper. Scripture keeps us focused on the new self. "Whatever is true...noble...right...pure...lovely...admirable—if anything is excellent or praiseworthy—think about such things" (Phil 4:8).

We Become What We Think

In his short story "The Old Stone Face," Nathaniel Hawthorne dramatically pictures how we become what we think. The tale centers on Ernest, a young boy who longed to see the legend of the stone face fulfilled. Sitting on their back porch, his parents explained how one day a great man would come to their village who would resemble the figure on the mountain that towered over their village. Ernest would ponder that face which had playfully been carved by nature.

Whenever the rumor spread that the great man had been located, Ernest was among the first to find out if it was so. It never was. During Ernest's teen years, there was General Blood and Thunder, but his face, hardened and cruel from years of battle and killing, was unlike the kind expression in the old stone face. Others came and went. Though in his lifetime the man of the stone face had not yet come, Ernest continued to longingly study the face, noting the humility mixed with strength, the love mingled with steadfastness of purpose.

By the time he was an old man, Ernest had built quite a reputation for himself. His loving service to his community had won him acclaim; his wisdom and maturity caused others to seek him out for help and counsel. One day an old poet visited the village just to bask in the splendor of this man, Ernest. After warm, animated conversation, the two old men walked slowly to the village park, where Ernest gave his usual Sunday evening lecture. The poet sat in front staring at Ernest as the old man began his speech. The setting sun lit up the stone face in the mountain behind Ernest. After glancing from Ernest's face to the stone face several times, the poet became nervous with excitement. Unable to constrain himself, he stood, interrupting Ernest's speech, shouting, "Ernest, he is the stone face. He's the stone face." The astonished crowd confirmed the discovery, but Ernest vehemently denied that he could be the man of the legend.

Whether he was or not didn't matter. The many years of looking at the stone face had slowly changed Ernest into the image he pondered for so long.

This is what Paul tells us in this chapter's Power Verse: by God's Spirit we will be changed day by day. Much of that change comes from constantly thinking about what we should be.

POWER ACTIONS

We suggest that you read this book more than once; perhaps make reading from it a weekly habit year after year until what you think becomes who you are. That's something you can do for you.

With your kids take a trip to the library to find "The Stone Face" and begin reading it with your children. Ask them what the story means to them and tell them what it means to you. Bring in the spiritual side and illustrate how we can be changed step by step through reading the Bible.

Even if you can't find "The Stone Face," ask your children to think of one thing they want to change about themselves. You need to come up with one too, as well as having a few suggestions for each child (i.e., yelling in the house, teasing a sibling, etc.). Tell them yours and ask for some suggestions on how to make some changes. Do the same with their change areas.

TEN

MANAGE ANGER

The One Who Makes You Angry May Be You

POWER VERSE

But now you must rid yourselves of all such things as these: anger, rage, malice....   COLOSSIANS 3:8

POWER LESSON

After preaching a sermon on anger, a pastor had scores of people confide in him that it was a major problem in their homes. He told me he was surprised. I would not have been. My counseling and teaching experience has convinced me that anger is one of the most destructive forces in our families. In surveys attempting to identify family problems, it's always near the top of the list. In one survey asking ministers' wives where they and their husbands most needed help in their families, over 60 percent put dealing with anger first.[1]

No wonder. The Bible points to anger as a major human problem. The apostle Paul associated it with our sinful natures, and in telling us to rid ourselves of it he used four different words: anger, bitterness, rage, and malice. Then, he threw in brawling and slander which result from anger (see Colossians 3:8; Ephesians 4:31).

Anger is not always wrong; it's a legitimate emotion. So Paul could say, "In your anger do not sin. Do not let the sun go down while you are still angry" (Eph 4:26). Anger, like other emotions, signals trouble and warns us that something needs to be done. It's an emotion that helps us protect ourselves and others. Even our bodies react; when we are angry, a rush of adrenaline hits our veins and makes us alert and strong.

Anger is part of being human. However, when wrongly motivated or expressed, it can be a terrible reaction causing all sorts of harm. "Anger is cruel and fury overwhelming" (Prv 27:4). It hurts others when we get violently upset with them without any cause. We make people feel like trash or like trashing us. The same is true when our fury makes us overreact or react in destructive ways. It's OK to get angry at a kid if he deliberately did something wrong; that shows we care and that we expected better things of him. But when it prompts us to punch him or call him names, the anger is obviously not constructive.

"Well, Dad. You have a new white car, now!"

Some people are chronically angry. The Bible calls them hot-tempered (see Proverbs 15:18). Being short on temper is a major-league struggle for some people. Inside them is a caged monster; they're never sure when they'll have an uncontrollable impulse to turn it loose. Sometimes they bottle up the anger and it solidifies as seething resentment. At times, the boiling anger spills over, scalding those it touches. The force is so powerful, and their control so limited, that when in a rage, some people feel that they are standing by watching themselves act, helpless to do anything about it. This is why some people blame demons for their behavior. Usually, however, it's rage that's possessing them, not a demon.

I sensed deep heartache in a middle-aged man who told me what this inner angry beast had done to his family life. His wife had defended herself from his outbursts by becoming indifferent and distant. His daughter hated him. "What can I do about it? I've been a Christian for decades, but I've never been able to control this thing," he said. I've heard this same plea from enough Christian men to know that short tempers are not in short supply.

Dealing with Your Anger

What is the answer? For starters, admit it. It's surprising how hard it is to see our faults even though they are plain to everyone around us. Anger is like this; we tend to justify it and blame others for "making us angry." Admitting the problem is ours, and taking responsibility for it, gets us to the starting line.

Second, recognize it may not be easy to deal with. Most of the people I talk to about this say, "I thought I would become a Christian and everything would be OK; and it was for a few months or years, but then…" They tried praying, walking in the Spirit and other spiritual maneuvers, and they were often discouraged.

Emotional problems aren't simply dealt with by a prayer. Certainly, trust in God is essential, but it needs to be coupled with action. And the Bible offers steps to take.

Determine what is behind your anger. If we start with the idea that Scripture says some people have more of a problem than others, then we can logically ask, why? Start with physical reasons. Medical science has pretty well concluded that anger can be linked to body chemistry. A condition called hypoglycemia, low blood sugar, can trigger angry outbursts; it releases into the system huge amounts of adrenaline, the hormone that prepares a person to fight and to face emergencies. With this chemical surging through his arteries, a person overreacts to the slightest annoyances. The answer to this condition lies in controlling the intake of sugar. A verse of Scripture or a prayer won't change your body chemistry... but a diet will.

Also, the chemistry in the brain may create anger. Researchers aren't sure what causes the problem, but they have established that there is some connection between the brain's physical condition and a person's emotional state. Before attributing a bad temper to your old nature or some satanic power, get a checkup. Besides a trip to church you may need a trip to your doctor.

Perhaps inflexibility makes you lose your cool. In the Hebrew language, being quick-tempered is compared to having a short nose or shortness of breath. The wise man in Proverbs 14:29 has a long nose (is patient), while the stupid person is short of breath (quick-tempered). The patient person takes a deep breath as he holds his anger in. A patient ruler (see Proverbs 25:15) is dubbed "the long of breath." The Hebrew word for temper refers to pliability in metal, which must sometimes bend or flex in response to conditions. As pliability is a strength to metal, it is a virtue to persons. All of this adds up to the idea that an ill-tempered person is one who is too unyielding. By remaining too rigid he breaks under pressure. To lengthen our temper (having a longer nose or taking a long breath), we must become more flexible. Much anger comes from trying to force our will on others. When they don't go along with us, we get upset. We have to learn to back off sometimes.

Ask yourself if you're too rigid, too demanding, and too unbending; that may explain your anger. Unhealthy families tend toward inflexibility. Members of families without emotional flexibility have poorer psychological health than those that are flexible. A man said that his father told his sister, who was pregnant outside of marriage, that he would never speak to her again, and he didn't. Occasionally he answered her phone calls, but he didn't speak unless he had to. He was a Christian man who thought he was taking a moral stand, but his unforgiving attitude caused his daughter terrible guilt and pain. The man's inflexibility created a troubled relationship and a troubled family. Being resentful, bitter, and angry is no way to solve problems. "Man's anger does not bring about the righteous life that God desires" (Jas 1:20). Check out why you are so unbending. Is something behind this, such as disappointment that life hasn't turned out as expected? A desire to shore up a sagging self-image (things have to go your way or else)? Guilt feelings? Fear that if you bend a little, you'll lose your convictions and morals?

Ask yourself if perhaps some other emotion lies behind your anger.

Some counselors suggest that some men substitute anger, an acceptable emotion, for emotions that are not.

For example, a man who didn't get an expected promotion at work is feeling disappointed, sad, perhaps frustrated and disillusioned. What he should do is to recognize these emotions and talk to God and someone else about them. Perhaps he should even take his wife's advice and get alone and have a good cry. Tear glands have no gender. Remember, great generals of ancient times cried publicly; Alexander did so because he had no more nations to conquer. But these emotions seem to be strangers to today's man; he's had little practice admitting and dealing with them. So what does he do? He feels an emotion that is allowable—anger. He lashes out at the boss or the company for not being fair, or even at himself for not doing better. Then, with this anger boiling at the surface, his wife or kids upset him and it erupts all over them.

Handling Anger

We men must get in touch with all our emotions. When angry, we need to ask if we should be experiencing another emotion instead.

Then we should verbalize our emotions. For whatever reason, it helps us cope with an emotion if we tell someone how we feel. A specific Bible verse doesn't tell us that but experience does. The Bible makes it clear that we should involve others in our emotional life. People help us get through grief; they comfort us when we are overwhelmed by frustration or fear. After all, we are told to "mourn with those who mourn" (Rom 12:15). How is anyone going to do that with us if we don't tell them how we are feeling? Besides, if we're feeling hostile, bitter, resentful, or even jealous of someone else, we are commanded to confess it. Being truthful about our emotional state is essential to dealing with it.

Instead of saying we are angry, we too often display that we are. Why do men slam doors when they're angry? To communicate with someone else. We often communicate our emotions nonverbally; we even learn to decipher these wordless messages. If he slams the door between the kitchen and the dining room, he's angry; if it's the front door and he walks out, he's really steamed. Why? It's safer. If we don't want to be caught feeling this way, we can always deny it. "You were upset with me last night when you stormed out of the house, weren't you?" "Who, me? No, I was just in a hurry." By such actions, we think we can get the person's attention and force them to take up the issue.

We express anger nonverbally because some of us aren't used to saying point-blank how we feel. If we did, we might reduce the emotion and prevent the negative reactions—especially those that are so damaging like insulting or hitting someone. If we can learn to say, "I'm disappointed in you," or, "I'm feeling frustrated," it will keep us from showing anger in ways we later regret. My wife and I have always had trouble doing this, but we finally caught on. When we first began to practice this, she once said to me, "I'm really upset with you." I immediately replied, "That's great. Let's sit down and talk." We did. At last we were learning to deal with each other's angry feelings.

There is one more practical step to take in handling anger—or any emotion. We should deal not only with what we are feeling but also with what we are thinking. Sometimes, we are enslaved to our emotions because we think we can't do anything about them; we think if we feel a certain way, we are going to act it out. We focus on the emotion.

However, the Bible places a lot of importance on what we are thinking. We are to be transformed by the renewing of our minds (see Romans 12:2). Applying this to our emotions, it means that when we are feeling angry, we should examine our thoughts. In some instances, it may be possible to change our feelings by changing our thoughts.

Study yourself a bit. Next time you are angry, ask what thoughts are going through your mind. What are you telling yourself? Perhaps it's a thought that triggered your anger and not a situation. Too often, we blame the circumstance. My daughter spends more money on clothes than I permitted her, and I get angry. My son walks out of the room when we are arguing, and I blow my top. The formula is simple enough: Event A produces Emotion B.

However, there is another way to think about it: insert another item in the formula—your thinking. Event A triggers Thought B which in turns provokes Emotion C. Now your perspective is quite different. It isn't the kid or the circumstance that is provoking your anger; it's what you are thinking about the kid or the circumstance. So to prevent the anger, you need to know what you're telling yourself. Perhaps you're saying, "My kid's headed for destruction because he won't listen, so I'd better be upset." Or, "My kid won't listen, so I must be a terrible parent and therefore I am angry at myself." Or, "If I get angry at my kid right now, he will listen to me."

In some circumstances, your thinking is wrong and your anger isn't justified. One act of disobedience doesn't mean your child is destined for tragedy. A child's disobedience does not mean you're a bad parent. You shouldn't be thinking that the way to control your child is by getting angry. Sure, it's OK to be angry, but there are better ways to get a kid to obey. Your message is incorrect and thus your anger is unnecessary.

Psychologists and physicians tell us that most men don't deal well with their emotions and they suffer for it. Their health is worse than a woman's, and their lives are shorter. Their families suffer too. Why not handle your emotions before they harm you—and others?

POWER ACTIONS

You need to get very practical with this issue. If you are struggling with severe outbursts of anger, make an appointment with a doctor. Find out if there is a chemical problem. If it isn't chemical, keep a journal of when you experience the desire to flare up. Write down what external circumstances surrounded the desire. Did you get enough sleep? Did you receive bad financial news? Is there a lot of stress at work? What did you just eat? Was it because you didn't get your way?

Once you have isolated these external causes, you are prepared to do battle. When you either recognize the cause or the effect working in your life, stop and get long-nosed, that is, suck in a deep breath. Next, meet with your mate and tell her what is going on. If it doesn't subside, tell your kids that you are feeling angry about something and need time alone. This will let everyone around you know about your emotional state and teach your children how to handle it.

"I give my Dad two every morning in his coffee."

"I think I'd like to contribute *this* spinach to the missionaries."

ELEVEN

ACCEPT CONFLICT

Add Conflict to Taxes and Death

POWER VERSE

It is to a man's honor to avoid strife, but every fool is quick to quarrel.   Proverbs 20:3

POWER LESSON

When I was working as an assistant to a seminary professor, one of my jobs was to supervise a teaching lab session and then evaluate the students who had done their practice teaching. When the prof, Howard Hendricks, evaluated the job I was doing, he pointed out one major weakness: I wasn't critical enough of the students' performance. "Be hard on them," he would say over and over again, but it was tough for me to be tough. When I asked myself why, I realized it was because I didn't like conflict. I even had some Scripture to back me up—at least I thought I did. Take the above verse: Doesn't it say it's honorable to shun dissension? Add to that other proverbs such as, "Starting a quarrel is like breaching a dam; so drop the matter before a dispute breaks out" (Prv 17:14).

I eventually came to realize that my dodging conflict was not based on Scripture but on something else. I didn't like clashing with others. In fact, I had learned as a child to hate it. There was so much of it in my home. Though my mother and father were never harsh with me, they were with each other—

because of my dad's drinking. Shouting matches were weekly occurrences. Often I cowered in my bedroom, covering my ears, trying not to hear them. It was during one of those moments that I resolved to never fight with others. I would be a peacemaker. But eventually, I learned that my attitude and approach were wrong.

God wants us to strive for peace with others, not by avoiding conflict but by facing it. All those verses that I used to justify shunning controversy never really meant what I thought they did. They advise us to avoid arguing, screaming, and fighting with each other, but they don't tell us to avoid all conflict—that is, if we carefully define the word. Conflict is something that occurs whenever two or more people have a disagreement about something and when they become obstacles to each other. Screaming insults at each other, violently arguing, and hitting are possible responses to these disagreements. Conflict we should accept; these negative, damaging reactions we should avoid. For example, the proverb "Starting a quarrel is like breaching a dam; so drop the matter before a dispute breaks out" is referring to such responses. The Hebrew word for quarrel indicates heavy-duty, angry disputing. If we don't drop the matter, we'll get into a dispute, or a legal battle. So, properly understood, the verse is saying, "Don't get into a heated argument and lose control; better to stop before someone hauls you into court."

Other Scriptures about conflict are similar; while warning us to avoid heated arguments and the like, they don't tell us to avoid conflict. We should get used to having conflict. It's inevitable in any relationship, simply because people are not alike. We have different values, ideas, needs, beliefs, and goals, and those differences will cause conflict in relationships when we are closely bound together as in the family. Marriage, someone has said, is like two porcupines sleeping together. The closer we try to get, the more likely we'll have problems adjusting. The more we try to work together, the more discord we are bound to have. We will become hindrances to each other in any area where we have to mutually share the use of space, money, time, energy, etc. A wife wants to go to a movie while her husband would rather stay home and watch a basketball game on TV. That occasions conflict. If we want to be together, we have to resolve this difference—and countless other ones.

The same thing will happen between you and your kids. Sometimes it happens over the use of space: if you want to watch TV and your teenage son wants to listen to the stereo, and if both of these electronic devices are in the living room, you have a conflict. You are bound to clash over money matters: when your daughter wants designer jeans and your budget calls for ordinary ones, you're in the middle of a contest.

Accepting Conflict

Speed Leahs, a business consultant, claims that the first step in handling conflict is accepting it. Those who don't will be handicapped, and Christians are high on the handicapped list. He discovered this when conducting a research project investigating churches that had fired their pastors. He wanted to find out why. Yet, over 60 percent of those he contacted refused to talk with him about their situation. From that he concluded that many Christians think that if they love each other, they won't have any conflict. When they do, they have neither the courage nor the skill to deal with it.

Conflict is part of any shared relationship. It is not always because we are sinful; it's simply because we are different. Look around the house and you'll find every room is a place for potential conflict. The living room—is it to be lived in or looked at? A husband may clutter it, thinking it's the thing to do; his wife may think otherwise. The dining room—should the mustard and ketchup be served in cute china or pewter bowls? Or is putting them on the table in their own jars good enough? The bathroom—should the toilet paper be rolled from the top or the bottom of the roll? Ann Landers reports that she has had more letters asking her about that than about any other subject. The bedroom—in cold weather, is it best to sleep with the window open or closed? This is definitely a hotter dispute than those we've mentioned so far. And clearly, there are other serious issues related to the bedroom. The point is that a husband and wife face potential conflicts, some humorously petty, some harshly profound, in all areas of life: religion, sex, money, work, parenting, relatives, recreation, etc.

The only way to avoid conflict is to avoid relationships. And, unfortunately, that is what some people do. Because they can't manage well the differences they have with people, they simply withdraw. I had a relative once who was harshly critical of the church our family attended. He didn't attend any church, protesting, "All they do is fight." To his credit, he was never once in a church fight. His way to handle conflict was simple: stay away.

This is what people who won't face conflict have to do. We can never get close to anyone if we aren't willing to work at the differences that would keep us apart. An intimate family is not one without differences, it's one that copes with them.

Prominent biblical characters had their share of strife with others. Moses, David, Jesus, the apostles—all were people of conflict. The apostle Paul even took on the apostle Peter, publicly confronting him. The Bible encourages us to face the issues we have with other people. "Better is open rebuke than hidden love" (Prv 27:5).

Just as strongly as the Bible affirms that conflict is OK, it warns that we should avoid negative and harmful ways of dealing with it. When your son wants to occupy the living room, or your daughter insists on buying those designer jeans, what do you do? Do you get angry, grouchy, or blow your stack? Scripture has a lot to say about these reactions. "Rid yourselves of all such things as these: anger, rage, malice, slander, and filthy language" (Col 3:8). Maybe you're always picking fights or escalating little skirmishes into major battles. The Bible warns against being an argumentative and ill-tempered man. Do you blame others for making trouble, bully to get your own way, belittle, or even hit? A recent Gallup poll learned that one out of twenty parents physically abuse their children. This is proof enough that many people resort to violence to solve disagreements in their own families.

Managing Confiict

It's crucial that you take some time to reflect on how you react to dissension. Comparing yourself to various styles of managing conflict is a good way to do this. Conflict management experts list five such styles and sometimes use animal names to label them.

1. *The Turtle.* This is the person who withdraws, either because he's afraid of conflict or considers it wrong. This results in his simmering underneath, thinking people ride roughshod over him and push him around. Like a pressure cooker, the tension builds up on the inside and eventually explodes, scalding everyone who is near.

Those who don't erupt are in a perpetual pity party. Some constantly feel sorry for themselves, demeaned and defeated because they let people, including their kids, walk all over them. And they rarely resolve issues because they are busy running from them.

2. *The Teddy Bear.* This person is somewhat like the Turtle; he dislikes conflict for the same reasons, but instead of retreating from it, he steps in and tries to smooth things over between himself and the other person. Teddy Bears want peace at all costs, and it usually costs them dearly. Nothing gets solved, and they get frustrated and sometimes angry, especially at those who want to deal with issues.

3. *The Shark.* Some people are called Sharks because they want to get their own way and will eat others up in the process. Always out to win, Sharks don't make good friends, parents, or spouses. Insensitive and inconsiderate, they often love to fight and dominate other people. They aren't willing to see other people's points of view and often fail to see any gray area in disputes. Sides are either right or wrong, and they are most often on the right side. For them, compromise is a dirty word.

4. *The Fox.* Not so for the Fox; compromise is his style. He gives a little to get a little. His tactic is much better than those we've mentioned so far. He is more ready to face conflict than the Turtles and Teddy Bears, and is willing to consider others. Compromise is often a very good approach to use, but it is not always effective, because it often deals with an issue in a superficial way. Take, for instance, the issue of the daughter's jeans. If the parents and the daughter too quickly come to a compromise, buying her the designer jeans if she pays half the cost, they may ignore some underlying issues that they need to talk through, such as why the daughter wants these clothes or what she thinks about her parents. Perhaps her clothes are a major attempt to overcome a poor image she has of herself, or perhaps she thinks her parents are cheap. In the process of considering what she should wear, the parents would be wise to deal with these issues as well. Foxes often fail to do this, and as a

result, they leave many issues unsolved.

5. *The Owl.* Owls, on the other hand, see issues as problems to be explored and solved creatively. They try to discuss the conflict, looking at all sides of it. Their approach is to sit down and talk about the issues in depth. If stymied, they will get a friend, pastor, or counselor to help them work through the matter.

Which of these animals are you? Keep in mind that any of these approaches might be acceptable in a given situation. For example, some issues aren't worth confronting, so you simply withdraw. You don't debate everyone who challenges you. And sometimes you have to be a Shark and seek to win, especially when there is a moral or spiritual principle at stake. Yet, if you find yourself using one approach most of the time, your ability to handle conflict is limited.

To change your style, it's helpful to look at what makes you the animal you are. Knowing why may show you that your approach is the one you used as a kid and that it really makes little sense. Many Teddy Bears and Turtles were bred in homes where there was a lot of shouting and fighting. Not only did they learn to hate the ruckus, but they never learned to deal with issues that caused it. Sharks also may have come from homes where there was a lot of anger and other negative responses to conflict. These people learned that if they were going to survive, they would have to fight. Shouted at, they learned to shout back. For this reason, abused children so often turn into abusive parents.

Maybe you fear conflict because you always want to please people. You may have little self-esteem and ego strength. This makes you a permissive parent who always gives in to your kids; you're afraid if you say no, they will dislike you.

Maybe your aversion to conflict is because you're afraid

you'll lose control and batter someone with your tongue or the back of your hand. Maybe you're a fighter; you thrive on dissension and are quite argumentative because you had to defend yourself when you were growing up. I know a man who's quite feisty; he grew up as a Protestant in a Catholic neighborhood where he was constantly harassed because of his religious views. Always having to defend himself made him quite argumentative, and he still is, even with his friends.

POWER ACTIONS

Conflict is never easy, but it is truly one of the inevitabilities of life. If there were only two people on earth, they would have conflict. We want to help you determine which "animal" you are. Begin by keeping a record of your conflicts for a week or two on a note card or in your daily calendar. When a conflict occurs, react as you normally do. After the conflict is over, write down how you handled it and what type of animal you were.

At the end of two weeks, look at your notes. Most likely, you'll discover that you are different in different situations. You might operate very differently at work than you do at home.

TWELVE

PLAN YOUR LIFE

Manage Your Life or It Will Manage You

POWER VERSE

Teach us to number our days aright, that we may gain a heart of wisdom. PSALMS 90:12

POWER LESSON

Breakfast finished, a farmer stepped out of his house and headed for the feedshed to get grain to feed the chickens. On his way he noticed a loose hinge on the feedshed shutter, so he changed directions toward the toolshed to get a screwdriver to use to secure the hinge. Not finding the screwdriver in the shed, he recalled leaving it on the tractor when the carburetor needed adjusting. So he walked to the field where the tractor was parked. Putting the tool in his pocket, he decided to test-drive the tractor. Riding toward the feedshed he spied a wagonload of hay he had intended to toss into the barn loft. Deciding to do so, he hooked the wagon to the tractor and drove toward the barn. Opening the barn door, he found it had several loose boards. Deciding to fix them, he ambled toward the toolshed to get a hammer. On the way, he remembered he hadn't yet fed the chickens. So he turned toward the feedshed to get the grain, and his wife called him for lunch.

Does this resemble some of your mornings? It certainly does many of mine. Unfortunately, this farmer's half day is much like some people's lives—cluttered with tasks begun but not finished, commitments made but not kept, and goals dreamed but never realized. They bounce from one thing to another, knocked around by circumstances like a helpless billiard ball. For them and the farmer, some planning could have changed all that. Instead of managing life, it manages them; instead of driving, they are driven. They do what they are forced to, not what they choose to do. They remind us of Paul's description of immature Christians who are "tossed back and forth by the waves, and blown here and there by every wind of teaching" (Eph 4:14).

The remedy for this is planning. The slogan "Plan your work and work your plan" is well known in the workplace. Now many men are applying planning techniques to family life.

Though the Bible doesn't contain all the principles you might find in a current time management book, it certainly recommends that we practice them. "Teach us to number our days aright, that we may gain a heart of wisdom," suggests we consider carefully what we do with each twenty-four-hour period (see Psalms 90:12). Life is short. We should have a lifetime game plan, being sure we strive for the goals God has given us. Christians have priorities to live by. "Seek first his kingdom," said Jesus (Mt 6:33). Time doesn't permit our doing everything we might be asked to do or want to do. We have to make decisions and budget our time and energy just as we do our money. Sometimes we must choose between the good and the bad, often between the better or best. Many worthy things must be laid aside for those that are more worthwhile. To do so we must devise daily and yearly agendas and attempt to stick to them.

Steps in Planning

Planning is a bridge between intentionality and reality. Here are some tips to help you use your time wisely.

1. *Set broad-based life goals, not just vocational ones.* Ask yourself what you would like to have accomplished when your life has ended. One way to do this is to pretend to write your own obituary or the epitaph for your grave marker. Try to include all dimensions of life: occupation, marriage, family, church, community, world, and personal life (physical, spiritual, social, intellectual, emotional).

2. *Evaluate these goals with two tests.* First, ask if they are as lofty as they should be. Perhaps you need to aim higher in some area of life that you have been neglecting. Second, ask if they are realistic. Here is where most of us err. We choose goals that we have neither time nor energy to realize, seeking to be and do everything. We fail to realize that we must do less in one area to do more in another. This creates an imbalance: we tend to pursue lofty goals in one or two areas and neglect the rest. Frequently, a man's vocational goals get the most attention, despite the fact that he may have high goals for other areas of his life. For example, when I ask fathers what they most want to have on their tombstone, 90 percent of them include the words: "He was a loving father." Yet, research shows that most of them haven't decided to sacrifice vocational goals to make that happen.

In a nationwide poll men were asked if they wanted to spend more time with their families. Most answered yes. Later, when asked if they would take a job that would give them a higher salary even though it meant spending less time with their family, they again answered yes.

This step involves seeing how demands and goals in different areas of your life will compete against each other.

Using your goals as lenses, look at your life. Which goals are you in the process of achieving? Which are you not? At this point, list as many as come to mind, even though you may not think you have the time to do something about them. For example, your vocational goals may require enrolling in evening school; goals related to your family mean spending more time with your daughter.

Make a list of all that needs to be done in your life. Give this process some time. You might take a personal retreat for a day or weekend to do this, including some quiet meditation and prayer in the process. Some men have an annual planning weekend with their wives at a hotel or a resort.

3. *Establish priorities.* Without this third step in the planning process, we would be emotionally crushed under the weight of the pressing needs in step two. Doing this third step makes life possible and livable. We establish priorities. We simply decide what can and cannot be done. Here we say to ourselves, "I won't fail to do something because I can't do everything." Then we choose what most needs to be done. Answering the following questions will help you.

- How urgent are the needs in this area? When must they be met? Now, today, soon, someday?
- How important is this area? Very, quite, somewhat, not so important?
- How often must the needs be met? Daily, weekly, occasionally, sometimes, seldom, not at all?
- Can someone else help me meet these needs? Yes, no, maybe?
- What will happen if this area doesn't get attention now? Disaster, trouble, difficulty, nothing?
- What areas need attention first and in what order?

By the time you're through with this step, you should have a list of things that need to be done and also an order of priority. Obviously, you should give attention to those that are most urgent. You may have to give up your trips to the health club temporarily to help your kid get through a personal problem. Or you may have to spend less time at work or with your family for a while to go to exercise, because if you don't your health will be at risk.

4. Set long-range goals. With these priorities in mind, you're ready for the next planning step: setting long-range goals. Turn this list of needs into goals that you want to reach within a certain amount of time. Some of your long-range goals may be accomplished in the space of five years, others within a year. Visualize where you want to be and write that down as something to strive for. At this point, don't try to state what you need to do to reach the goal, just visualize where you want to be within a given space of time. For example: "Vice president of my company; closer to my son, Nate; a better small group leader at church, etc." This puts you in a place to think about how you might reach these goals. It also gives you something concrete to pray about.

Now determine how you are going to reach these goals. Ask what things you have to do to get closer to your son or to become the vice president or to be a better group leader. To get closer to your son, for example, you may decide to discuss with him what he would like to do with you and schedule weekly and monthly times with him. In some planning schemes, these tactics are called objectives. That is, you write them down as things you want to accomplish: "During the next month I will have several discussions with my son about doing things together."

Once you have this list of objectives for each area, you can prepare your schedules: yearly, monthly, and weekly. Thus, the hours and days of your life are now given direction; going bowling with your son on Tuesdays, or buying and reading a book each Saturday morning is directly tied to your life goals.

5. *Stick with the schedule you made.* The last step may be the most difficult of all: working your plan. This requires the discipline to stick with the schedule you've made. For that you'll need to stay near the Lord and trust the Holy Spirit. And you'll have to keep revising your plans by going through the whole cycle on a regular basis.

Planning to Succeed

Whenever I talk to people about planning, I almost always have to answer two objections: "It takes too much time, and I don't stick to my schedule anyway." The first is partly true; it does take a lot of time. Besides the time you probably spend at work planning, you'll have to spend three or four hours a month doing personal planning. Yet, those hours are well spent. The time required to plan will be more than redeemed by the time you no longer waste because you do. Remember the farmer?

As for the second protest, "I never stick to my schedule anyway," my answer is a question, "Does your life have more order and do you accomplish more because you have a schedule, even though you don't follow it perfectly?" Our purpose in planning is not to make us perfect but to make us better. Anyone is bound to do better with a plan than without one. Thus the slogan, "Those who fail to plan plan to fail."

Ivy Lee, a business consultant, knew this. Years ago, Charles Schwab, president of the Bethlehem Steel Corporation, gave him a task: "Show me a way to get more things done with my time, and I'll pay you a fee within reason." Immediately, Lee handed Schwab a sheet of paper with these instructions, "Write down the most important tasks you have to do tomorrow and number them in order of importance. When you arrive in the morning, begin at number one and stay with it till it's completed, then begin number two. If any task takes all day, never mind. Stick with it as long as it is the most important one.

"If you don't finish them all, you probably couldn't do so with any other method, and without some system you'll probably not even decide which one was most important. Make this a habit every working day. When it works for you, give it to your staff. Try as long as you like. Then send me a check for what it is worth."

Several weeks later, Lee received a check for $25,000 from the steel executive, who included a note saying it was the most profitable bit of advice he'd ever been given.[1]

The most important thing in life is to do the most important things in life. Planning will help you do that. Plan to plan.

POWER ACTIONS

Goals! Answer these questions: Where do you want to be by retirement? Where do you want to retire? Where will you be in ten years, five years, one year? Are you going to help your kids through college? Will there be money to help them buy their first house? Do you want to live close to the grandchildren? How do you want to spend vacations? Are there special lessons that you want your children to learn?

When my wife and I moved to our most recent church position, our daughter was entering high school. We knew it was going to be hard on her to attend a new school without any friends. We set one goal for that period of four years—to make sure that Becca had a quality high school experience. As each situation came along, we asked, "Will this improve the quality of her experience? How can we be supportive in order to assure the quality of the experience?" When she graduated as the school's top English and drama student, we could look back at our goal and say, "We accomplished it." We knew where we were going and we knew when we got there. What are your goals as a father?

Setting goals accomplished two things: my daughter got a better father, and I knew that I had done what I was supposed to do.

"You'd better hurry up and fill in that new calendar because everyone else already has a plan for your life."

CAPABLE COMPANION

PART THREE

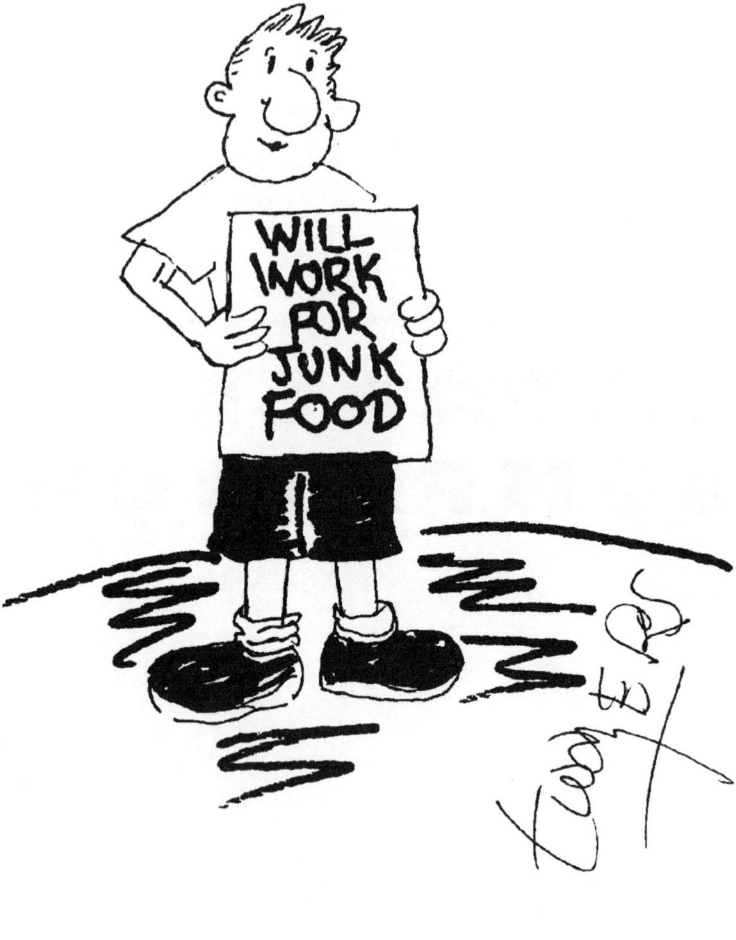
WILL WORK FOR JUNK FOOD

THIRTEEN

SEE THE VALUE OF CONVERSATION

Talk May Be Cheap, but It's Valuable

POWER VERSE

Speaking the truth in love.　　　　　　　EPHESIANS 4:15

POWER LESSON

The father of one of the girls at the camp had just died. The youth leader asked one of the speakers at the camp to go with him to deliver the bleak message to her. He explained to her that her father had died of a heart attack and that someone would accompany her on her return home. Her gasp and her questions signaled her initial disbelief, then the tumultuous flow of tears signaled her shock. They stood by silently, waiting. Finally, still struggling for control, she said haltingly what must have been among her first thoughts, when she realized she would never see her dad alive again, "My father... I never really knew him." It was a statement of finality and regret. Now she never would, and she felt denied.

We seem to have a built-in yearning to know our parents; in our modern world, it's fathers who most frustrate that desire. We men are much more private than women, less willing and able to tell others what's going on inside us. "Besides," we say to ourselves, "living in the same house, eating at the same table, using the same bathroom, our wives and kids have plenty of chances to get to know us." The problem is that they don't know what's inside us; they have to guess, mostly because we don't tell them. As one wife said, "You have been such a wonderful husband these thirty years, Harold, but I still can't help wondering what you are really like."

This mysterious peculiarity of American fathers makes us somewhat lost to our children. Because of this a Harvard sociologist entitled his book about dads *Finding Our Fathers*. In the book, he quotes one grown son whose craving to discover was constantly thwarted by his dad's inability to communicate.

> My father gave me a ride back to the airport yesterday; we were alone together. The whole way there I wanted to talk to him, make some connection with him, hear how he felt about me, talk to him about all that's happened between us. But he hardly said anything to me. We just drove out there in silence.[1]

Perhaps it was less his father's willingness to talk than his inability. From the father's point of view, I know how laborious it can be to share myself with my children. Despite countless games of Monopoly and scores of fishing trips with them, I still found it hard to discuss serious subjects with my kids. I was envious of the freedom Ginger had to interact with them. With her they talked openly while plopped on the kitchen counter, feet dangling, comfortable, and at home. Why was it so different with me? Why did I feel this barrier?

The barrier was not outside us or between us; it was inside me, like a wall. With other people at other times, the door of my heart would swing open and there would be liberty for things to come and go. But somehow with my kids, the door would be shut and the things inside I wanted to get out were trapped in there and I just couldn't say them. When I tried, I felt so uncomfortable it came out sounding distorted. The frog was in my heart, not my throat.

To overcome this handicap, I had to first realize how important it was that I learn to be more transparent with my kids. Talk is one of the greatest tools we have in our Power Dads toolbox, and we need to learn how to use it.

Teaching them about God requires more than superficial conversation with them. In Deuteronomy 6:6-7, parents were told, "These commandments that I give you today are to be upon your hearts. Impress them on your children. Talk about them when you sit at home and when you walk along the road, when you lie down and when you get up."

Insert God's Word into your daily conversation. That's the import of the words "Talk about them." Too often we expect our kids to follow our values because we live them out before them. This is true, but just as we need to walk our talk, we need to talk our walk. While spiritual truths are transmitted through our actions, it is our words that give those actions meaning. A study of families done several decades ago found that kids tended to follow their dads' values when the dads talked about them, not just lived them.

We fathers need to talk about ourselves, our feelings, dreams, and longings. We have to reveal our true selves, which requires our being open and honest. Scripture says a lot about this. Only if we are truthful will we be known. Paul urges Christians to speak the truth in love and warns us to put off falsehood and speak truthfully (see Ephesians 4:15, 25).

This doesn't mean we have to tell our kids everything we are thinking. To be intimate doesn't require our being psychologically naked, as if people need to know all about us. Some things are best kept to ourselves. There are times when we need to tell our kids we're afraid or worried. At other times, this would only burden them needlessly, when they need to be assured by our strength and courage.

Nor does honesty require that we be impulsive, as if to be transparent we need to immediately share a thought or a feeling. We should think before we speak. The apostle Paul made this clear, "Do not let any unwholesome talk come out of your mouths, but only what is helpful for building others up according to their needs, that it may benefit those who listen" (Eph 4:29). Before I speak, I should ask, "Will this be edifying?"

But most of us men are prone to say less, rather than more than we should. And we need to learn to be more transparent with our kids.

Being honest also makes us more credible. It's hard to believe people who never tell us of their doubts, weaknesses, or fears. We will be more believable if we admit we're human and that we ourselves struggle.

Filling the Emptiness

Sharing ourselves shows our children that we love them. When we entrust our inner selves to someone, we are giving them the most valuable gift we have to offer—ourselves. Kids feel loved when we confide in them. When we don't, they feel distant and even empty inside.

Most of my life I felt that way about my father. But when I was in my forties, after feeling distant from my own boys, I realized my need to feel closer to my dad. I came to see how superficial our conversations were. Phone calls were about the Pittsburgh Pirates or the weather or his latest woodworking project. The deeply significant things never found their way into our conversations. The fact that we had so little closeness was my fault too. I left home for college and never returned to my hometown except for occasional visits. I sensed little need to relate to him and failed to recognize any reason he might have to relate to me. I phoned once in a while, wrote an occasional letter, exchanged Christmas gifts.

I wanted more, and a time came when I sought to do something about it. Seated on the small commuter plane that bumped its way above the Appalachian Mountains, I made a resolution[2] which marked the beginning of a new era for me. I sat beside an older brother, also from the Chicago area, who with me had rushed to catch this plane after our sister's urgent phone call, "Dad will probably not live long. You had better come while there is still time." On that plane, I resolved to break through to him, to somehow have some moments with him that I could call "personal."

When my brother and I walked into the hospital room, the usual awkwardness was there, but it was also clear that Dad was delighted to see us. We talked about little things, and then, summoning my courage, I began to talk about our past family life, something I rarely did with him or even with my brothers and sister. Reminiscing had been absent, either because there was too much pain or too little closeness. Now we talked of Kennywood Park and the roller coasters, the picnic grounds, and other pleasant places and events. Our most intimate moments had been riding the roller coasters and Ferris wheels, or when we gathered around a radio listening to Jack Benny or Bob Hope.

Suddenly, there in his hospital room, Dad injected a statement about his drinking. It was sort of an apology. I was too startled and unprepared to give much of a reply. This was something none of us ever discussed with anybody. Now, after decades of silence, an eighty-one-year-old man brought the matter up with his sons. Was this his unfinished business? I mumbled something in reply like, "That's all right." I wish I could have said more, but when I left that room, I floated. It was one of the most remarkable moments of my life. And it didn't stop there, since my father lived for two more years and we had other moments of deeper sharing. We even prayed together.

There are many reasons why we might have trouble communicating with our kids. In his research on men, Michael E. McGill discovered that many of us have come to depend on our wives to talk for us.

In many families, relationships between father and children occur through the mother. One woman of forty-two described her relationship with her father. She said:

> Even now, when I have a grown family of my own and I'm not dependent on Dad for anything at all, I still communicate with him only through Mom. Whenever I call home, I always talk to Mom. It's kind of awkward when she's out and Dad answers, because we just don't have anything to say to each other. It's usually, "Hello, your mother's not here."
>
> "Tell her I called. Goodbye."
>
> Mom writes, but Dad never does. Every now and then she makes a point of telling me how he reacted to something I or one of the kids did, like, "Your father thinks you did the right thing about your job." Or, "He sure is proud of those grandkids." But I never hear it from Dad himself. It must be that he needs Mom to talk to me as much as I need her to talk to him. It would be simpler if we could talk to each other, but we never have been able to, and at this date it's not likely that we are going to start. I imagine we'll

just keep on talking through Mom. When she's not there anymore, we probably won't talk at all.[3]

Fathers need to communicate directly; our kids need to hear from us. Break the pattern of talking through your wife and start speaking to your children.

During a coffee break at a men's seminar where I was speaking, one of the men told me what he had just done. He admitted that what I had said about not talking directly to children was embarrassingly true of him. So, he went to the phone and called his grown daughter. "Her first response was, 'Hi, Dad, what do you want?' Obviously I never call to talk—only when I have some piece of business. I replied, 'Oh, nothing, I just called to say that I love you and to talk a bit.'"

He said nothing else, but the slight smile and moist eyes told me how good he felt. Perhaps we fathers need to connect with our children as much as they do with us. Just do it.

POWER ACTIONS

Do you have any old photos around the house? One night, dig them out and talk about what you remember that happened on the days the pictures were taken. The pictures will bring back stories and feelings that you had as a child. Your kids will get an inside look at the person they call Dad at the key point when you were their age. This will allow them to understand you better, because you have gone back to their experience level. Let them ask you questions about their relatives. It is quite amazing what can happen.

On one trip back to the homeland, my daughter asked my mother to show her my old pictures and other family photos. We learned all about our family heritage, and I discovered some wonderful things about Mom. The same things will happen for you.

"A support group, Pastor? As you can see, I've got all the support I need right here."

FOURTEEN

TRY TALKING

Finding the Lost Art of Conversation

POWER VERSE

These commandments that I give you today are to be upon your hearts. Impress them on your children. Talk about them when you sit at home and when you walk along the road, when you lie down and when you get up.

DEUTERONOMY 6:6-7

POWER LESSON

Mike, a friend of mine, related to me how he wished his father had been more transparent and communicative. Though loving and hardworking, he kept his feelings hidden. Mike told of a few incidents that gave him a peek into his father's inner world. The day Mike left home to enter the Army, during the Vietnam war, he saw his mother and dad waving good-bye, standing on the driveway, tears rolling down his mom's face, dad with a stoic, grim expression. "I wondered then how he felt about my going; I could guess, but I really couldn't detect exactly what was going on inside him," Mike said. Years later his mother solved the mystery. "After I left," he explained, "she and my father went up to my room to change the bed. They both broke down and wept for a long time. I cherish the thought of my dad being so moved by my leaving." Of the mental pictures of his father, that one of his father crying aloud in his room was among the priceless ones.

He continued, "When I was in Nam, I received a letter from my father, the only one in my whole life. He didn't really share personal feelings; it was mostly about what he was doing and wondering about me. I've got that letter in a bank safety deposit box."

Though sparse, his father's self-disclosures were sacred to Mike. We may say talk is cheap, but in a child's memory, a loving father's personal words can be priceless. Are you depositing personal words to remember in the bank vault of your child's heart? It's not difficult to do—if you follow a few tips.

Tips for Talking to Your Kids

Start early. Babies and toddlers need fathers. Much has been written recently about the process of kids bonding to their parents. Being around to say "Boo" when your children are young will make it a lot easier to say more meaningful things to them later.

Spend time together. The notion that quality time is a replacement for quantity is a myth. It takes time to get close. People don't blurt out deep, significant things quickly. Getting into heavy stuff takes some warm-up time. Writer Paul Tournier said that small talk can lead to meaningful talk. It takes some chatting to reach a comfort zone; we need to chat about easy subjects before we get to the riskier ones.

Share in activities that prompt talking. Watching videos, attending sports events, and the like may help us relate to our kids, and we ought to do them. But hiking, sitting around a campfire, or building a boat together may do more to stimulate meaningful conversation. Kids feel more at ease talking while they are doing something with us. They are not all comfortable with direct, face-to-face conversation. Adults and kids generally communicate indirectly. In a doctor's office waiting room or on a bus, we can promote conversation by "getting something between ourselves and the child"—keys, wallet, or a magazine.

Give thought to what you can do to foster meaningful dialog. Taking walks seems to do it; somehow moving our legs together gets our tongues going. Working together promotes this kind of indirect discussion. The fact that family members do so little work together may be a major reason why our relationships are shallow. One sociologist says that one of the appliances that has hurt family communications more than any other is not the TV set but the automatic dishwasher. While he may be kidding, he makes a good point. Washing and drying dishes together used to be the setting for a lot of family fellowship. That was true in our house, especially with my wife and our two oldest children, who worked and talked together in the kitchen. When either of them visits, they still go to the kitchen to talk with their mom.

Watch for happenings that open the door to deeper dialog. After you've watched a video that has stirred your emotions, ask your kids to discuss their feelings, and then share yours with them. If you've had an emotionally gripping experience, talk about it. I saw a father do this when I was riding in the car with him and his two boys. I had known them only the few hours since they picked me up to take me to a church camp outing where I would be the speaker. I quickly noticed that the father appeared to have a wholesome relationship with the two sons, one a teenager. Coming to an intersection, we saw an accident happen right in front of us; one car hit another violently, shoving it off the road and into a field ahead of us. As we passed the spot of the collision, we saw a woman slumped against the steering wheel of her car, head bleeding. Several cars had stopped and people were on their way to help her, so we continued on our trip, all of us emotionally shaken and silent.

Then the father wisely started us talking. He described what he had seen, how the whole episode had seemed to happen in slow motion. Then he described his reactions of alarm and fright. This led the kids to describe excitedly their own observations and feelings. What followed was a sort of debriefing session, all of us therapeutically talking out our emotions and reactions to a traumatic situation. And in the process, that father was tightening his emotional ties to his sons.

Take the Risk

If you're not used to sharing the deeper part of yourself, you'll not know exactly when to do so and may be more cautious than you should be. To do so, you'll have to go beyond your own comfort zone, and this can be risky. You can make it easier on yourself by avoiding big jumps at self-revelation. Try sharing what is a bit threatening; cautiously inch your head out of your shell. This has worked well for me. At the supper table, for instance, I've thought of something I could say that normally I wouldn't have because it would have been slightly uncomfortable. Then I've said to myself, "Why not?" and forced myself to spout it out. Usually, the response from my wife and kids has been rewarding and my fears of looking ridiculous unfounded.

We should especially risk talking about some subjects that promote closeness, which is exactly why they are so threatening to those of us who fear intimacy. Describing your nighttime dreams is one way to share yourself. This is something my wife and kids do very well, but which to me is tantamount to walking outside in my underwear. I just hate to describe a silly, confusing dream, and yet, I keep struggling to do so. Also, tell your kids of your personal struggles, visions of the future, ideals, mistakes, and embarrassing moments, even though doing so may be terribly intimidating. In the process, urge your kids to respond; ask them if they ever felt or thought the same. Once in a while, after you've shared a problem, struggle, or personal goal, ask for their advice or opinion.

Talking directly is most important, but there are other means of disclosing who you are. Leave a message on the answering machine. Write a note and pin it on the family bulletin board; it could say "Thanks" for a job well done. Send a greeting card or a note in the mail. Include a letter or note saying things that it might be difficult to express in person. Your kid may tuck these away to keep as precious heirlooms of a father's affection.

POWER ACTIONS

Take your kids to breakfast or do a "power lunch" with them. As my daughter was growing up, I would take her to breakfast before school once a week. We would plot out her plans for class projects, talk about my work week, and I would always say, in my western Pennsylvania accent, "How's your spiritual life doing?" To this day, even though she's off at college, my wife and daughter mimic my accent and say to me, "How's your spiritual life doing?" My actions led to her openness about her daily life and her spiritual life. We talked. We still do. It all began with those once-a-week breakfast meetings.

Find a day and time that works best with your schedule and your children's. Make the date, write it into your daily planner, and when someone asks to meet you simply say, "I've got a very important breakfast on my schedule for that day." Now that she's at college, we use e-mail several times a week, just to say hi and talk about what is going on.

"Sure, son, you can do bypass surgery on me."

FIFTEEN

LEARNING TO LISTEN

How to See with Your Ears

POWER VERSE

He who answers before listening—that is his folly and shame.

PROVERBS 18:13

POWER LESSON

"Chick, you've just promised Larry a new bicycle!" My wife's startled voice and three kids' loud laughing jolted me as I sat at the supper table, where my thoughts had drifted from the family's conversation to my job. I was caught once again—not listening. Larry had asked for a bike, and I absentmindedly said, "Sure."

Despite my poor record, I know how important listening is. Ed Seely's research tells me that. Seely asked teenagers what they most wanted in a youth leader and a parent. The top of the list, far above everything else was this, "I want someone who listens to me; someone who understands my concerns." My not listening is as habitual as writing with my right hand; I'm getting better, but it's taken decades of concentrated practice. With turtlelike speed I've reached about forty yards of a 100-yard dash.

The Bible doesn't say a lot about listening, but it places a high value on it. "Be quick to listen," says James 1:19. In the same breath James says to be "slow to speak and slow to become angry." The implication is that if we are swift to listen, we might be in less hurry to lose our cool or say the wrong thing.

I've learned this from my wife, Ginger. When she heard bad news, her first reaction was to ask questions and learn more about it. My impulse was to get upset and blurt out some response. My kids knew this, and when they had a problem, they took it to her first. They also learned that when they did approach me, my first reaction wouldn't be the final one—that after I thought about it and learned more, I would change my mind. "Listen first," says James.

Besides keeping you from losing your temper and saying the wrong thing, listening will help you show your children you're interested in them. This is one of the major reasons children want their parents to hear them. "Love me—hear me," they figure. Wives also think this way. And when their husbands don't listen to them, they feel rejected. Many women have told me, "I don't share my feelings with my husband anymore because he just doesn't care how I feel."

In a rather humorous way, I discovered how people feel good about your listening to them. It was on a long airplane trip. Starting a conversation with a man next to me who was also flying from Hong Kong to L.A., I learned that he had just completed a very fascinating job. He had just led a crew of people to cut a huge ship in half. It had been grounded, and the only way to salvage the engines and the important parts of the freighter was to use explosives to cut the floating half free. I asked questions, and he seemed delighted to tell me all about his work—how they had lived on the freighter for six months, mounting and wiring the explosives to every bulkhead inside and outside the freighter, calculating carefully so that they would go off at the same moment. I was riveted to his account of the details of this amazing operation. Then he pulled from his briefcase a scrapbook of pictures of other jobs he had done, including demolishing huge buildings.

I listened to him for hours, at least half of our long flight, genuinely interested. But I was also hoping for a chance to share my Christian faith with him. None came. During the whole time, he learned nothing about me except my interest in his work. He never asked me one question about myself—my occupation, my reason for being in the Orient or even my name. Yet, when we were embarking from the plane, he shook hands and said, "I fly a lot, but I want to tell you that you have been one of the most interesting persons I have met while flying." Of course, I was interesting to him because I was interested in him.

Ways to Listen

Listening is one of the most unselfish things we can do. And this is why we don't do more of it; most of us are rather self-centered. There are more people looking for someone to listen to them than people looking for someone to listen to. Paul Tournier, prominent Christian counselor, said it well: "Each one speaks primarily in order to set forth his own ideas.... Exceedingly few exchanges of viewpoints manifest a real desire to understand the other person."[1]

Yet, as someone has joked, God obviously wants us to listen more than we speak because he gave us only one mouth but two ears. Maybe that's why we have to practice twice as hard to use the two of them. Yet, it takes more than using your ears to be a good listener.

For one thing, you have to listen with your posture. Ever have a little kid, even as young as two, get upset because you're not looking to him when you talk? I've had them grab my face and turn it toward them or slam dunk the newspaper I was holding in front of my face. Kids want to be noticed; they want us to show that we're listening to them and not just nod or grunt while we continue to read the paper or watch TV.

Good listening is, at its core, thoughtful concentration, especially about two things—what your kid is thinking and what he is feeling. When she says, "Daddy, I don't like school," delay your lecture about the long-term benefits of education and find out what she means by "don't like." Not liking school can mean lots of different things, from being afraid of a particular teacher to the pressure she feels from studying subjects difficult for her. You need to learn more facts and discover more about her feelings. The bottom line may not be what's happening but what she's feeling. If you miss that, you'll miss the real problem.

Whenever your kids say something, see if you can identify the feeling behind it. They won't always come right out and tell you what they're feeling; you'll have to try to deduce that from their words and actions. If they say, "Oh, Dad, do you have to go to work today?" ask what emotion is lurking behind that statement. The next suggestion can help you do this.

The best listeners know how speaking is involved in listening. Those who don't may give a quick answer, make a swift judgment or change the subject. Wise listeners say what will keep someone on track and help the person explain more fully. They do this by asking lots of questions. If their kid asks, "Why can't we buy a new computer?" they ask, "How do you feel about having a new computer?" To get someone to expand on what they are saying, they say, "Tell me more," or, "What happened next?" Or you help them evaluate what they are thinking or feeling by asking, "Why do you feel this way?"

or, "Why do you think you are not as capable as Jimmy?" Some questions aim at getting a person to understand better what he's thinking or feeling: "Do you think you are angry? Or are you really discouraged about what happened?" or, "Are you certain your teacher expects that?"

A major verbal tool of good listeners is "reflective listening." The concept is simple but extremely effective. It's a way of avoiding a thoughtless reaction as well as gaining more understanding. When the child complains, "I don't know why Mrs. Craig gave me a D on that paper," a parent resists the temptation to scold the child for complaining or to rise up in defense of the teacher. Instead, he simply repeats what the child has just said, using other words, "You don't see what Mrs. Craig saw about your paper that made her give you a D?" The parent keeps on doing this with everything the child continues to say. So, if your daughter says, "I don't want to go to Sunday School because the teacher is boring," you reserve giving your opinion and instead just repeat back what she said, "Your teacher is not interesting and therefore you want to stay home today?" This does three things. First, it gives her the feeling that you've really tried to understand her. Second, it helps you understand by giving her more opportunity to explain what she means. She may reply, "No, Dad, I don't want to stay home; but I just don't want to go to my class." You now grasp better what she meant in the first place.

Third, this gives your child a chance to think through things for herself. Sometimes, people don't want us to give an answer; they merely want us to listen. We are a sounding board that helps them think aloud and come to their own conclusions. Because we listen, they get an opportunity to "get things off their chest." If all we do is dispense advice, we will miss the opportunity to help our children evaluate things themselves. When this technique works, the conversation will be similar to the following.

Johnny stomps into the house and says, "I am not playing with Billy anymore; he is so selfish."

You refrain from pointing out your own child's self-centeredness and simply repeat, "You are not going back out to be with Billy because he only thinks of himself?"

Johnny says, "Right. I wanted to play cars and he wants to play that dumb new game he got for his birthday last week."

You reply, once again stuffing the strong desire to point out the game is or is not dumb, "You don't have a good opinion of Billy's new game, but you would rather play what you want to play?"

"Yes," your son continues. "He never wants to play what I play."

You reply, "You think that Billy always plays what he wants to play?"

"Well, not always, Dad. Sometimes he does what I like to do."

"You mean that Billy doesn't always demand you play what he wants to?"

"Yes, I suppose he does do what I want to do once in a while."

"So, Billy doesn't always only play what he wants to?"

"No, Dad. He just wants to play his game now; I suppose I could do it with him for a while, even though I think it's a dumb game. S'long, Dad, I'm going out to play with Billy."

Now, I don't guarantee it will always turn out like that, but I can guarantee you that you'll improve your listening 1000 percent if you practice this with your kids. In the process you'll be of tremendous help to them. Of course, this is only one way to listen and is not to be used all of the time. People don't want us to sound like parrots. Sometimes they want our opinion, ideas, and advice—but only after we've heard them.

We dads would do well to follow the advice of the warning sign and STOP, LOOK, AND LISTEN.

POWER ACTIONS

Decide that the moment you walk into the house you will start putting your listening power into operation. Really try to show you're hearing what your wife or kids are saying. Observe their reactions and how they treat you in return.

The next evening, come home and act as if you are passively hearing things as you read or do the work you've brought home. Observe their reactions. Did they treat you differently? Which way made you feel like an engaged, active, and maturing father? It probably isn't that hard to predict the answer but you need to experience the difference. It will make the lesson and the homework much easier.

Family T-shirts that say it for you.

SIXTEEN

UNDERSTAND HOW KIDS THINK

Little Adults They're Not

POWER VERSE

Train a child in the way he should go, and when he is old he will not turn from it.   PROVERBS 22:6

POWER LESSON

The results of Emerson Eggerich's research surprised him. He was studying Christian men who were known to be good fathers. He wanted to find out what they were like. Topping the list of their good traits was this: they understood their children. Eggerich hadn't expected this. After all, these men weren't all psychologists or educators who had studied children. These extraordinary dads were mostly ordinary guys: farmers, mechanics, carpenters, and the like.

Yet, they knew kids. They treated their children appropriately for their age: they didn't demand more, were sensitive to their needs, and took into consideration the children's concerns.[1]

Good fathers are like tailors who fit their clothes to the person who will wear them. No pattern fits all sizes. It's quite possible that this is what the famous proverb suggests, "Train up a child in the way he should go and when he is old he will not depart from it." The phrase "way he should go" could otherwise be translated "according to his way." The unusual

Hebrew wording could mean that when you train a child, consider his individual peculiarities, inclinations, and age. The more you personalize your training, the more likely your kid will not depart from it when he is old.

This is what the great sculptor Michelangelo did with a piece of rock. It was said that when he looked at a block of marble, he could see a statue inside of it. We dads should try to see what our kids are like and try to shape them accordingly.

Essentially, this means that we should not treat all children alike and that we should certainly not treat them as if they were already adults. The Bible recognizes that kids are kids; they talk, understand, and reason like children (see 1 Corinthians 13:11). Good dads remember this when they deal with them.

Eggerich said he didn't know how these good fathers learned what kids were like. Perhaps they got their sensitivity from observing how their own fathers treated them. Or else they were good observers; they watched kids and listened to them to see just what they were like. Some of them, no doubt, read about kids or studied them in college.

Understanding Our Children

However we do it, any of us can learn to understand our children. We have to start by recognizing that kids think differently than adults. About age six, children learn to reason. This is why this year is called "the age of reason," and why most civilizations start formal schooling then. Before this, they don't fully understand cause-and-effect relationships. Ever see a kid spot a squirrel at the park, then see another squirrel hours later far from the first and think it's the same one? It's the same reason they can believe in Santa Claus, even though he keeps on showing up in one department store after another.

Kids just don't put their world together in a reasonable way. To them the world is mysterious, magical, and fanciful.

This means that you don't sit down and reason with a four-year-old. It won't hurt to do so, but you should not expect him to understand. So, when you're disciplining him, you should not expect him to grasp the idea that if he walks out on the street he may get hurt. Eventually, he'll learn that, but not by your sitting down and explaining it to him.

Recognizing how children think will help you do a better job of teaching them. Developmental psychologists, such as Jean Piaget, propose that young children are not capable of understanding many of the abstract and figurative concepts of Scripture until later in life. Since they are used to hearing adults talk about things they don't understand, they usually just let them go by. And to adults, their misconceptions are sometimes funny: "Draw a knife on God and he will draw a knife on you," is the way one child understood the King James rendering of James 4:8, "Draw nigh to God and he will draw nigh to you." But some misunderstandings can be confusing and hurt a child. What pictures of God are etched early in a child's mind? How do children mentally process the God of Sinai who thunders from the mountain, threatening that anyone who touches it will die? Describing this biblical scene, an overzealous and dramatic Sunday School teacher might send some children home trembling and confused. Through close, informal conversation with their children, parents can uncover these misconceptions and right them.

Also, avoid using symbols and metaphors that children can't understand. Kids are like aliens in an adult world—they see things from their point of view and they are quite literal. They misunderstand a lot, like the little boy who drew a picture in Sunday School. When the teacher asked, "Tell me about your picture," he explained that in the backseat of the airplane were Jesus, Mary, and Joseph; the man in the front was Pontius the Pilot. And of course, the picture was about the flight to Egypt. If you say, "Jesus is the door," they think of something with a doorknob, that you can knock on and open. Light, for instance, comes in the form of a light bulb, candle, or flashlight. What then do they think when we sing, "This little light of mine; I'm going to let it shine"? They do not have the capacity to understand that this means that if they do good things and are nice kids, they will be good witnesses for Jesus. The same is true for a concept like being "fishers of men." Somehow children realize we aren't really going to cast our lures into the lake in hopes of hooking people, so they just let it go by as they do a lot of stuff they hear from adults.

To talk with young children, use concrete terms. Don't talk about shining as lights. Simply explain that if they act properly, God will get credit for their behavior and it will make other people notice him. Explain that Jesus will forgive them and live with them if they receive him, rather than, "If you open your heart, Jesus will come in." They won't understand either the concept of "heart" or the idea of "opening."

When your kids get to be six or seven, they will start to better understand these metaphors. Yet, you should still be careful not to use them without carefully explaining what they mean. For example, the parable of the wise man building a house on a solid foundation is still beyond their grasp. When they hear it, they will understand that Jesus is probably not talking about the construction of buildings. But they won't grasp that he's talking about living their lives based on his sayings. They'll have to be twelve or thirteen before they can reason that out. At that point, watch out; early adolescents love to argue and debate, simply because they have learned how to do it. It's as if they have a new tool they want to practice using, and they will constantly use it on you. Practice with them, even though you will tire of arguing and discussing issues with them before they will. They need to expand their abilities.

Respect a child's limited ability to reason. Children can't figure things out as we can. They can't always know that if they do *A*, *B* will happen. So, we respect their right to have accidents that we adults might have foreseen and avoided. Or take the matter of remembering. Arriving home late, a seven-year-old says, "I forgot." We may be tempted to accuse him of lying. But, in reality, he really didn't remember. David Elkind, the leading American child development expert, claims that even twelve-year-old children normally have such lapses of memory. Keep in mind that your child's memory may not be as sharp as yours. If your child fails to come home on time, it's possible that he did forget. You may be tempted to think this is just an excuse. But you would be wise to give him the benefit of the doubt and go easy on him. He'll be glad you did, and eventually so will you. Blessed are the kids whose dads understand them.

POWER ACTIONS

How do we learn to understand our kids? Practice listening, and if you don't understand something they've said or a question they've asked, ask for an explanation. Each time you ask, you'll learn a little more about them. So the next time you are with your kids, ask questions, "Why did you say that?" or "Why did you do that?" Say it as if you want to learn. Believe me, they'll be willing to tell you.

And don't forget that they don't understand or do things the way that you would. Do not get frustrated when they don't perform a task or answer a question the way you wanted. When that happens it is time for you to ask a question that will help you understand the inside of a child's head. But watch out for cartoon characters, fairytale people, and modern myths, because they're all inside that little head as well. It does get crowded sometimes.

"Honey, I'll be done in a minute. I'm just preparing for the breakfast table conversation with the kids."

SPIRITUAL TEACHER

PART FOUR

"Where did your mother and I go wrong?"

SEVENTEEN

BE THE SPIRITUAL LEADER

Build a Solid Foundation

POWER VERSE
Fathers, do not exasperate your children; instead, bring them up in the training and instruction of the Lord. EPHESIANS 6:4

POWER LESSON
Bad news can sometimes alarm and comfort us at the same time, as the results of a recent national survey did. The question: "Who was the greatest spiritual influence in your life—pastor, youth leader, father, mother?" Far and ahead of everyone else was mom. Dad was so far down the list he was hardly worth mentioning.

That is bad news for Christian fathers. And my guess is that most fathers regret this because it creates in them more than a gram of guilt. After all, we know Scripture says a great deal about fathers bringing up their children "in the training and instruction of the Lord" (Eph 6:4).

In shaping our children's spiritual lives, we ought to be doing our fair share. In fact, we should be taking the leadership. And the majority of Christian women I know would cheer us if we did; they are generally the home's spiritual leaders by default, not by desire.

Impacting kids spiritually does require someone taking the lead. Husbands and wives often are confused about who should initiate spiritual activities. They each expect the other to do it, and when no one does, nothing happens.

Fathers ought to be taking charge. I don't mean making a pious assault on your wife and family, seizing control, and demanding people shape up spiritually. Being a spiritual leader involves taking the initiative in creating a spiritual climate in your home. Your wife should be involved, since Scripture makes it clear she is also your child's spiritual mentor (see Proverbs 6:20). Bring up the subject with her, discuss what should be done and then do a bit of planning for your kids' spiritual training. Decide which one of you is going to be responsible for carrying out the plans. It might be wise to divide up the tasks, assigning family devotions to one of you, holiday rituals to another, and so forth.

Realize that training and instructing kids in the Lord does not require force-feeding faith to them. Acquainting them with Christ is your responsibility; accepting him is theirs. You need to offer them sufficient data to make a wise decision and enough freedom to make it for themselves. One wise father told his children, "Your mother and I are Christians; we are going to teach you what it means to be one. We hope and pray you will choose to follow Christ. You must make your own choice and not simply be a Christian because we are. When you are old enough to decide for yourself, we will respect your decision, whatever it is."

Give Your Family a Spiritual Foundation

It's hard to overstate the contribution of a spiritual foundation in your family. Your belief in God helps you and everyone else in the family maintain a proper perspective about life.

Daily you have to resist the secular viewpoint that presses you to believe the world revolves around you. "There is no God; there's just you; you're number one; go for the gusto; you only go around once; you deserve it; do it your way; just do it." This viewpoint makes it tough to accept life's challenges and crises. With God as part of life, you have a dimension that transcends yourself. It counters the secular message with the truth that there is something beyond you and your family. Making God a part of family life relieves the pressure to always succeed or to milk all the pleasure and excitement you can out of every single minute.

Your spiritual outlook will better enable you to handle crises. A crisis can be like a battering ram to a family, putting strain on relationships, sometimes forcing them to collapse.

Whether a crisis will strengthen or strain a family will depend upon how it is handled. I am not suggesting that simply praying together will get you through all circumstances. Facing a crisis is much more complicated than that. But if you continue to draw on spiritual resources together, you will be better prepared to handle it. "Cast all your anxiety on him," says Peter, "because he cares for you" (1 Pt 5:7). As you do so, you may find yourself drawn together by fortifying each other's faith and hope.

Trusting in God won't make us welcome crises, but it will help us accept them. We'll know there's more to life than one setback, no matter how major it is. And we'll recognize that sometimes God allows them to test us or to cause us to grow.

A spiritual dimension in the home can also unite a family. Family loyalty will spring from being more like-minded, sharing the same values, dreams, beliefs, and ideals. Being spiritually one will make you more personally one.

Think of a triangle, with God at the top angle and each of

you at the bottom ones. The more each of you moves toward God and his will in the center, the more you move toward each other, even though total agreement is probably not possible or even desirable, since our differences enrich our relationship.

Think, too, of how much you can learn together. The wisdom you gain from Scripture and other sources will enable you to face life in harmony, instead of being at odds with one another.

There is still another way your spiritual leadership will enrich your marriage and family life. I discovered this during a communicating exercise Ginger and I were doing. She was telling me which of the ways that I showed my love to her meant the most. Having been married for twenty-three years, I was not expecting any surprises, but her answer not only surprised me, it shocked me, "When you pray with me and show concern for my spiritual life, that tops the list."

Never before had I thought of my initiating our spiritual times together as an act of love. I looked at it as a duty, something I was responsible to do. This new insight dramatically changed my perspective toward our spiritual oneness and provided added motivation to cultivate it.

A Christian leader told me about a man who had begun teaching the Bible to his young daughter. She told her friend about it. To her own father, the friend said, "Daddy, will you teach me the Bible like Emily's father?" That little girl's plea hit hard. The most loving thing we can do for our children is to leave them an inheritance of faith.

Recognize Your Walk Is Your Talk

To successfully pass on your faith, you will first need to live it. My eight-year-old son was on the second floor screaming for his mother, who was in the backyard out of earshot. I was in my basement study trying to work. Finally, frustrated by his shouting, I yelled as loudly as I could, "Howie, don't yell in the house."

A week or so later, all of a sudden a little voice in my head said, "Do you realize what you did the other day? How dumb to yell at someone not to yell!" When Howie again called for his mom, I changed my tactic. I walked across the cellar, up the stairs, through the kitchen and hallway, up the stairs into his bedroom, and I whispered, "Howie, don't yell in the house."

Scripture makes it clear that there is power in modeling. To Titus Paul wrote, "In everything set them an example by doing what is good" (Ti 2:7). Warning church leaders not to lord over those entrusted to them, Peter said they should be "examples to the flock" (1 Pt 5:3).

Modeling, Not Acting

Good modeling, of course, is not acting. We must not pretend or show off our good behavior. If our example is going to be effective it has to be honest. Kids see through us if we pretend to be up when we're down or glad when we're sad. They don't respect hypocrites any more than we do. One thirteen-year-old boy was talking to me about his dad. "He's easy to talk to," he said, "I like him. One day he was teaching us from the Book of Acts in our Sunday School class. Ananias and Sapphira were liars, and God didn't like that. My dad said, 'I don't want to be a phony.' That really changed my mind about him—I thought all adults were phonies. But not my dad. Now that I know that, we have a good relationship. When I have a problem, I go to him and know that he will be honest with me."

By being unreal, we not only lose our kids' respect, we also forfeit a good chance to teach them. Kids need examples of how to handle the negative things of life. We need to show them our depression so they can accept and deal with theirs. We ought to be open about our conflicts with others so they can manage conflict themselves. One Christian father told me his grown children said to him, "Dad, you taught us how to succeed, but you didn't teach us how to fail." Letting them be aware of our faults, struggles, and failures can teach them how to cope with life.

Modeling will also be made more effective if your child observes you in many types of situations: working, worshiping, praying, kidding around with your friends, relating warmly to your wife.

One final word. Modeling is not enough. Sometimes, parents make the mistake of thinking that if they just live out their beliefs and values, their kids will adopt those beliefs and values. Not so. Our kids are exposed to many examples, and they may identify solidly with some of them—a peer or a sports hero or rock star. If you're a good parent you have a statistical chance of being the most influential person in your kids' lives, but you should also try to expose them to other people who exemplify your values and lifestyle—teachers, youth leaders, missionaries, relatives, and friends.

We've seen the importance of trying to bring other adult Christians into meaningful contact with our kids. When my son Howie completed an application to work at summer camp, he asked us to look it over. On one line, he was asked if youth leaders had any influence on his life. He wrote, "Not only youth leaders, but many Christians in my church have had an influence on me." Your child will someday say that too—if you help make those relationships happen.

POWER ACTIONS

Search through your data banks. Where have you been dishonest in the way you live? Take that to God and ask his forgiveness. The next step is to start making some changes. Your wife and kids want the honest and real you.

A lot of us struggle with seeing ourselves correctly. Remember, we may not be able to see our foibles and hypocrisies, but our kids can. Pick out one area that needs some work and start on that one. Make it an easy one so you can see some quick results. Then try another. The next thing you'll know, the kids will be excited to be with dad, and mom will walk around smiling and saying, "Wow!"

"You have the right to remain silent."

EIGHTEEN

SHAPE A CHILD'S VALUES AND TEACH INFORMALLY

Cooperate with Your Kid's Best Teacher

POWER VERSE

God disciplines us for our good, that we may share in his holiness.... Discipline produces a harvest of righteousness and peace for those who have been trained by it.

HEBREWS 12:10, 11

POWER LESSON

My sons and I did a lot of hunting and fishing together, so much so that they became avid anglers and hunters, going far beyond my expertise. At times, when I saw how consumed they were by this sport, I regretted that I had introduced them to it, wondering if I should have spent more time in other forms of recreation or in more serious endeavors. I especially felt this way when one of them was not doing well in college. He passed his courses, but he was not highly motivated to succeed in any particular field—except field and stream. He spent endless hours reading hunting and fishing magazines and often headed for the lake early in the morning. I asked myself, "Where is the love for study and thirst for knowledge that my wife and I have? Why didn't I do more to pass those values on to him?"

During one of these regretful moods, I talked with the president of the college my son was attending. "Not to worry," he said. "You'll be surprised by the discipline, character, and skills your boy is developing through his dedication to outdoor activities." He told of his own grown son who at one time had devoted himself to a hobby, while being quite average in other areas of life. Eventually his devotion to his hobby had prepared the way for his college success as well as later excellence in his vocation. The president assured me that perfecting skills in an activity like fishing can produce some very valuable character traits and positive values. His insights were reassuring to me and they turned out to be true. Today, my son has transferred to his vocation and his role as a father the skills, attitudes, and values he learned from fishing: self-discipline, ability to study and observe, persistence, patience, and more.

Shaping Their Experiences

Children learn from any and every kind of experience. What they do teaches them more than what they hear from us or are forced to study. God knows this. As a faithful Father, he trains by sometimes allowing us to go through unpleasant experiences. Tough times can result in righteousness. Fathers who realize this possess an important tool, if we can call it that, for sculpturing our kids' character. We can shape them by shaping their experiences. We have the power to guide them into experiences that will produce the virtues and traits that will prepare them for life.

Let's suppose you want your child to be more responsible, remembering to do what's expected of her, not having always to be told to do something or do it the right way. Think of what you can design: suggesting she get a pet or join a school activity that will require some accountability. Base your choice on her interests and abilities. Children don't have to excel in everything they do to gain a sense of personal responsibility and self-discipline. Maybe she needs to be in a serving project or pursuing a hobby. Perhaps she needs to be exposed to people who model responsibility. Character is usually more caught than taught.

When I was in college, a very wise person created an experience for me that changed my life. At the time, I wasn't even aware of what she was doing. I complained about having to study classical Greek, even though I elected to do so, since it would prepare me for studying the New Testament in seminary. I was having trouble with Greek grammar and felt it rather useless to read passages about Greek generals who fought battles over two thousand years ago. So I griped to everyone who asked how school was going, including a Christian woman who was head of the Pittsburgh Child Evangelism Fellowship. Being a volunteer teacher in one of her clubs, I was invited into her home for dinner one evening. Over a delicious spaghetti dinner, I met another man she had invited, a doctoral student from a local university. His field of study was the Greek language, and we talked for hours about classical and New Testament Greek; he was a brilliant linguist. I left there impressed and inspired, as excited about studying Greek as I had been over eating that delicious spaghetti dinner. In one evening, my hate for Greek had been turned to love. Yet, I never realized what that woman had done until many years later. By then I had lost contact with her and was unable to say thanks for being so cunning. We fathers should be so wise!

Use the Walk-Talk Approach

I've had a number of men tell me their fathers were the major spiritual influence in their lives and then quickly add: "It wasn't because of family devotions; we had them, but they didn't help me all that much. It was our conversations; I learned a lot from talking to him."

Teaching our kids doesn't require giving them scintillating lectures or conducting creative family devotions. Many dads don't have the talent or training for doing these things, and kids aren't always eager to cooperate. Though there's room for some formal teaching in the home, the Bible also stresses the informal. Lesson plans and lectures are fine for schools, but classrooms don't have what's so unique to family life: a place of total living together, which gives parents the opportunity to teach anytime, anyplace, and do it in the context of real living.

This is precisely what we read in the Bible's most crucial passage about the home's spiritual training. "These commandments... are to be upon your hearts. Impress them on your children. Talk about them when you sit at home and when you walk along the road, when you lie down and when you get up" (Dt 6:6-7).

"So, how are you going to draw a spiritual lesson from this, Dad?"

You teach by constantly talking about God's truth, anytime, anywhere. Casual, unassuming, spontaneous, daily conversation is a powerful form of education. In fact, it's probably more powerful than a more formal type of teaching. That runs the danger of being too intellectual and unrelated to life. If that's the only time and the only way we talk about God, children can become saturated with words about Christianity without an opportunity to experience them. They may know a lot of Bible stories but have no idea how they affect their everyday life. When you inject discussion about spiritual things into daily life, it's much less likely to seem bookish and academic.

Way to Walk-Talk

So, how do we do it? First, of course, we should work at creating conversation, but we should also give some thought to how to insert spiritual truth into this conversation. This should be done naturally and appropriately, not artificially, making it appear insincere. Most modern kids won't appreciate a parent who is always popping off with Bible verses in King James English. I experienced this once when I was staying in someone's home. Walking into the kitchen in the morning I heard, "Good morning, Dr. Sell. This is the day the Lord hath made and we will rejoice and be glad in it." I was a bit stunned. Everyone else says something like, "Good morning, Dr. Sell, did you sleep well?" Though I respected this elderly woman, I didn't respect her greeting. I am not impressed by such contrived piety, and I think most kids would be impressed even less.

It's important that God's Word come across as genuine and relevant. To do this we might make Scripture part of an affirmation. To a five-year-old we might say, "You were kind to her, Eddie; that's important since the Bible says, 'Be kind to one another.'" Or we could include Scripture when giving an answer to a question or problem, "I struggle with worrying too: I find that praying helps, since the Scripture tells us to pray and not be anxious about things that bother us."

At times, we may use Scripture and spirituality as a basis for a rebuke. Both the Old and New Testaments approve of reproving adults as well as children, but we should be careful not to turn God into a heavenly policeman. Nor should we use Scripture to control a child without giving him a reason. "Because the Bible says so," is not much more effective than, "Because I told you so."

Some occasions inspire talk about God: viewing a sunset, hiking through a scenic forest, or looking up at the stars at night. These give you a chance to talk of God as Creator and to stress his care and faithfulness.

Find analogies from life, too. Jesus constantly taught this way. Telling us not to worry about having enough to eat, he called attention to birds and said, "They do not sow or reap or store away in barns, and yet your heavenly Father feeds them. Are you not much more valuable than they?" (Mt 6:26). And pointing to wildflowers, he said that if God would make them so beautiful, he would clothe us (see Matthew 6:28-30). There are countless parables that draw from ordinary daily life: the foundations of a house, a tree, a small seed, a wasteful son. We can do the same, taking advantage of what we and our children experience together.

A simple statement will do, such as "The way we talk to each other about our fears and problems is how we can also pray to God. He wants us to tell him about our struggles." Sometimes, we may elaborate more fully on the similarities of our experiences with spiritual realities. At Christmas time we can explain how our giving gifts to each other compares with God's giving to us.

Another way to insert God's word into our talk is to take advantage of questions our kids ask. Throwing a question at us may mean the child is having one of those golden "teachable moments." She's ready to learn. It's great to be around when that occurs. Schoolteachers love it; their problem is that they are often required to answer questions students haven't asked. That's what puts parents in such a good position to be teachers. Kids ask questions when they face problems, or their curiosity is aroused by something they heard or experienced. Living prompts questions, and parents are usually the closest persons around to answer them. Research shows that even a preschool child will ask thousands of questions during a year. Parents can watch for them and then share God's truth.

Children often ask questions casually because it lowers the risk level. When troubled, yet afraid to ask for help, they may subtly work their questions into a conversation. When one of my sons was thinking through a sensitive matter, he popped a question to me while we were shooting baskets in the driveway, "Dad, how do we know the Bible is true?" (swoosh). "I mean, wasn't it written by ordinary people a long time ago?" (swoosh) "Well, son, that's a good question. I'm glad you're thinking about—oops, missed—such important issues." I went on to discuss the kinds of things we talk about in a seminary classroom right there in the driveway. I knew from what he said a few days later that he had jumped a major hurdle in his life; for the time being he would trust the Bible and keep working on the issue of its truthfulness and authority. Every dad can be a teacher if he'll just talk.

POWER ACTIONS

In order to have informal teaching opportunities, you need to have some informal times together.

What things do you enjoy doing? Is it basketball? Playing catch? How about a board game? A drive in the country? A walk in the park or the woods? A craft? What is the best day of the week for some fun with the kids? Pick one or two or all of the suggested activities, but make sure that you have at least one informal time together every week. Although every day is ideal, life isn't. Sometimes they will just happen, so look for informal teaching times, no matter where you are. Some people call it "quality time." Once you are in the informal period—that makes it sound so formal, doesn't it?—listen and watch. The lessons will come, but don't force them. In the meantime, you're having fun with the kids.

NINETEEN

CREATE RITUALS

Welcoming God into the Kitchen

POWER VERSE

Blessed are those... who walk in the light of your presence, O Lord. They rejoice in your name all day long.

PSALMS 89:15-16

POWER LESSON

"Before we go to work in the morning, my husband and I pray for each other, especially remembering any special challenges we might face on that day."

"At the supper table each evening, we all share the best thing that happened to us during the day. It puts us in a positive frame of mind and helps us learn what the kids are experiencing."

"Each Christmas Eve we sit around the Christmas tree and discuss the Christmas story. We choose not to read it but to talk about what happened and what it means to us."

The above statements describe "rituals." For you the term might conjure up images of lighting candles or reciting the Apostle's Creed in a worship service. Not all rituals are necessarily religious, nor are they done only in church. A ritual is simply a routine activity, an accustomed way of doing things. For example, we usually have a habitual sequence of activities

"Hey, Mom, where did you put my biology speciman?"

related to getting up and going in the morning: coffee first, then shower, then breakfast, then dress (or is it dress, then breakfast?), perhaps jogging or reading the newspaper, etc. Even our conversation becomes ritualized, "Good morning; did you sleep well?" Rituals show up everywhere: saying goodnight or good-bye (kiss and hug, or just kiss or hug?), eating meals, making love, etc.

Once these things become fixed in our lives, we expect them to happen, and when they don't we feel out of sorts. Think how you feel when you miss your morning coffee, lunch, dessert, or evening paper.

Everyone has rituals, some daily and weekly, or special occasion ones like holiday celebrations or weddings. Family rituals are just regular routines the family started and became accustomed to doing. For example, they learned to wait till everyone came to the table before starting to eat; Dad always prayed, or other family members took turns, sometimes holding hands. After a while, no one has to remind them what to do, they just automatically do it. Often, we aren't even aware that we have a ritual.

Many of the rituals we adopt are those we learned in childhood. We can also devise rituals intentionally. One of the choice opportunities you have to guide your family spiritually is by creating rituals for celebrating, worshiping, praying, and learning about God.

Everyday Rituals

Let's start with daily and weekly rituals and then describe suggestions for holidays. It doesn't take a lot of effort to inject a spiritual flavor into some rituals. You need a little imagination and some time to plan. In a survey of couples, we found the following:

"Pray, holding hands, before meals."

"Pray in the car before starting on a trip."

"Thank God for safety after a trip."

"Discuss a sermon's impact after the Sunday service."

"Pray together out loud before going to sleep."

"Listen to Christian music after getting up."

"Read Bible stories at mealtimes."

"Sing songs in the car."

"Read a Bible verse and pray with the kids when we tuck them into bed."

"Pray with my child before I send him off to school."

A weekly ritual many Christian families do rises from a Jewish custom of giving a blessing on the Sabbath. It's a simple but very special and warm expression of love for God and for each other. Before or after an evening meal once a week, someone is assigned the role of giving a blessing to every other family member. For example, if it's Dad's turn, he turns to one of the kids and says, "I bless you for being such an encouragement to me this past week." Then to his wife he may say, "I pray for you that the very busy week ahead will go well for you." The blessing can consist of a prayer or an affirmation. It gives us a chance to bring God into each other's lives as well as to show we care about one another and recognize the good each of us can do. By passing the task around, we teach our children to be sensitive to other family members' needs and to be positive about them. Imagine what happens to an eight-year-old boy who has to spend the week thinking of some blessing to bestow on his ten-year-old sister.

Rituals can be directed toward any of the so-called "spiritual disciplines" of celebration, worship, study, or prayer. For example, note the rituals associated with riding in the family car. Before we set out for a trip, we pray for guidance and protection (prayer); during the trip, we take some time to read a Bible story book (study); after arriving, we thank God for our time together and for our safe arrival (worship and praise).

Holiday Rituals

Holidays and other special days can also be occasions for some rich and meaningful rituals. These times of celebration offer opportunities to learn about God and to worship and praise him. We suggest you plan to include some spiritual activities in your observation of major holidays and anniversaries: Christmas, Easter, Thanksgiving, and birthdays.

Moments with God at these times can add a wonderful spiritual seasoning to all the customary festivities: special food, colorful decorations, singing, joking, fun, and fellowship. You'll no doubt need some earnest discussion with your wife in order to modify your holiday rituals. People enter marriage with different ideas about celebrating and, sooner or later, end up debating what it means and how to do it, particularly over practices related to the major holidays of Christmas, Easter, and Thanksgiving. Arguments about things designed to lift our spirits—special foods, the Christmas tree, gift giving—end up dampening them. The sources of these disagreements are, of course, lodged in our memories of childhood family traditions and rituals. Since rituals have enormous sentimental value, we would like to continue to practice them, but they may be incompatible with our partner's family rituals and so we have some conflict to deal with. Compromise is one way to resolve these issues, each giving up some practices and accepting some of our spouse's.

You can, of course, concoct your own rituals, starting your traditions and creating activities that fit your family. With a little imagination, you can invent customs and establish habits that will saturate your lives with rich and meaningful celebration.

It is often somewhat difficult today to inject time with God into our holidays, even the ones that were originally designed to be spiritual, because they have become so secular. Our Thanksgiving festival seems to be more about eating turkey than praying. Associating Christ with Christmas and Easter may even be somewhat difficult, with the emphasis our culture places on Santa Claus and the Easter Bunny. Spending time with God can seem oddly out of place amidst the feasting, gift-giving, and football games.

Yet, it need not be. We can easily include God in our partying. And when we do, two important things happen. Our spiritual activities add something profound and meaningful to our festivities. And our partying puts a joyful tone into our relating to God. Of course, the place to start is to involve your family in church programs during holidays. Then you consider ways to add a spiritual touch to your home celebrations.

Stopping to praise God for his gifts to us before we open our Christmas presents can add a very special dimension to Christmas. To get kids to appreciate the spiritual emphasis, you need to make sure what you do isn't boring. Make it something they can participate in. Better to have them act out the Christmas story than try to keep their attention while you read lengthy passages of Scripture.

Kids really get into the type of ritual we've included in our Thanksgiving holiday time. We have a brief worship time after our turkey dinner. In it we include our "Guess What We're Thankful For" game. First, I pass out slips of paper giving something to every family member to do in the worship service. For example, I may give a slip to my daughter Becky that tells her to begin our worship time by praying. Howie is to pick out a hymn for us to sing. Ginger is told to find a Scripture passage to read. Everyone takes a few moments to prepare, and then we begin. At one point, I announce that we are going to share what we are thankful for. We each make a list of six things we are thankful for. These are then placed in a hat and redistributed. One person reads a list and we try to guess who wrote it. After all lists have been read, several of us lead in prayer. Not only is this fun, but it is also sometimes quite emotional, as we find ourselves on a list of what someone is thankful for.

To stimulate your own creativity, consider another couple's

Thanksgiving ritual. "We have a prayer tree. Out of a paper bag we cut a tree shape and post it on the wall. We make several leaves out of construction paper, and when we hear of a specific request or need, for ourselves or others, we write the request and date on a leaf. Then we establish a time for praying regularly 'through the leaves.' When a request is answered, we paste that leaf on the tree. At Thanksgiving we take the leaves off the tree and thank God for his answers to each one and for his faithfulness throughout the past year."

Another couple told us of their New Year's Eve ritual. "We spend time reflecting on the best and worst aspects of the previous year and giving thanks for them (that they happened or that they are over) and for the year that lies before us, that we can learn and grow from our past experiences."

"Honey, quick, get the camcorder. He just spit up."

For birthdays, invite people to pray sentence prayers, thanking God for the birthday boy or girl, right before singing "Happy Birthday" and lighting the cake's candles. In our family, we've shed a lot of happy tears doing this. As far as possible, try to match your spiritual activity with the purpose of the festivity. The sentence prayers at the birthday party are another way of affirming someone, which is the goal of the celebration.

The big advantage of starting family rituals is that they become traditions. Everyone comes to expect them, and there is no need to prod or push the family to do them. Granted, when your kid becomes a teenager, he might resist. But when he's married and has his own children, you'll no doubt find his family doing them. Spiritual rituals are powerful ways to make God real to your children. Don't be at home without them.

POWER ACTIONS

Certainly, we don't have to inject a prayer or recitations of a Bible verse into every family activity. We are being "spiritual" when we do the right thing or are being kind to each other, not just when we are talking about God.

Choose one or both of these:

1. Think of how you might insert some spiritual ritual into your family's daily or weekly schedule and talk it over with your wife.
2. Talk with your wife about modifying a holiday ritual to include some time with God.

TWENTY

CONDUCT FAMILY DEVOTIONS

A Contemporary Design for the Family Altar

POWER VERSE
We will tell the next generation the praiseworthy deeds of the Lord.   Psalms 78:4

POWER LESSON

Ever hear of the family altar? It's an antique expression that refers to a family devotional time, usually involving reading the Bible and praying together. For many years, this practice stood as the norm for healthy Christian families. Today, not many Christian parents are familiar with the term. I actually know a guy who, after hearing it was good to have a family altar, went to a Christian bookstore to try to buy one. If surveys are to be believed, the practice is about as out-of-date as the name that describes it. Few Christian families have regular family devotions, and those who do have not always found them to be an effective means of influencing children spiritually. Though many Christians are grateful their parents had regular devotions as a family, many Christians are not. I know people who say they are Christians today not because their parents had daily devotions with them but in spite of it. They came close to hating those times.

As a Christian father, you'll need to decide whether or not

you will have regular family devotional times. To help you answer this question, I suggest you distinguish between having devotions and intentionally teaching your children about the Christian faith. When it comes to teaching your children about spiritual matters, the Bible gives you no option. It puts a lot of emphasis on informal, casual teaching woven into your interaction with your kids in everyday life. By talking about God, just as you would about how to use a saw or multiply numbers, you make the Bible relevant. If you rely too much on a special "family devotions" time, you run the risk of being too bookish in your approach to God. Some educators contend that the child is saturated with words about Christianity before she or he has had an opportunity to understand those words experientially.[1] Forcing children to concentrate too heavily on the intellectual content of the Christian faith may give them a distaste for God.

Yet, while the informal approach is effective, you ought also to consider intentionally teaching your children; that is, to set aside time to share biblical truth and deal with spiritual issues.

Children are badly in need of knowledge. Spiritual ideas are not hiding inside them, like undeveloped photographs that slowly appear like Polaroid prints. Nor do children merely get ideas from experience, as if the only way for them to learn is to knock their heads against life's concrete. Children need wise teachers, and their parents are to be their first and foremost ones.

Yet, teaching wisely isn't easy. Some parents who are trained as teachers still aren't sure how to go about making the sessions interesting to children. If your devotions are tedious and boring, you run the risk of making them think Christianity is too. Making devotions interesting to your kids does not require genius, but it will demand some creativity.

How to Do Family Devotions

1. Provide Christian books and cassettes to be used by your children during devotions or any other time. Teaching formally doesn't demand turning your home into a school. The key to this is to supply your children with resources that deal with spiritual matters. There are effective ways to teach that don't require sitting down to a formal family devotion time. In a Christian bookstore or church library you can obtain books, audio and video cassettes, and other resources that will appeal to your child. The stories, lessons, and songs in these materials are as palatable as sugar-coated cereal. I've seen children wear out these books and recordings while digesting life-changing ideas. The easiest way, and one that is profitable for your children, is to simply read to them.

2. Vary your purpose. Your family devotions need not always be a study time to learn something new. Keep in mind the spiritual disciplines I mentioned earlier: worship, celebration, prayer, and study. Sometime you may simply want everyone to share something good that happened to them and then have a time of thanks. Or you may want to share what you most appreciate about God and then spend a few moments praising him. Having devotions doesn't always require reading from a book or from the Bible.

Do what's best for you and your family. Learn from other people, but don't try to copy them. Singing together may work well for some families, but not for others. Some men are great storytellers and can hold kids' attention captive by telling Bible stories in their own words. Others aren't and should rely on reading Bible storybooks.

3. Make devotions regular. Determine the best time and place and try to stick with it. But don't panic if there are interruptions, and adjustments in schedule have to be made. Better aim for something and hit it once in a while than to aim for nothing. You'll have to decide whether you think devotions should be daily. Many families we know choose several days a week, some only one day.

Of course, you have to select a convenient time. For many, suppertime is best, usually afterward. Bedtime is also good. Our kids loved our reading the Bible and talking about God at bedtime; they discovered it was a great way to postpone going to sleep as well as to spend time with us. They often drew me into lengthy discussions until I realized what they were up to.

4. *Keep them simple.* Don't make devotions so complicated that there's too much preparation; it makes them hard to maintain. Do something that you can get to and do easily—read from a good book, read a Bible passage and ask the kids a few questions, or do some informal sharing and praying.

5. *Make devotions time short.* Being brief may be the best way to keep devotions from the borders of Dullsville. This doesn't mean they will all necessarily be short; you may get going on a discussion that lasts for quite a while. The point is, let that happen if it does, but don't plan for it.

6. *Plan ahead.* Keeping devotions simple doesn't rule out some planning. Someone has to choose what book will be read or what part of the Bible you'll study and how you'll do it. Perhaps you can spend a devotion period planning later ones with your wife and kids. Let them make suggestions. During a visit to the bookstore together, the kids can help you choose books and other resources. You might even plan for different things for different nights: Tuesday is a missionary story, Thursday a Bible story, Saturday is an informal discussion.

7. *Allow for participation.* Though this sounds simple, the principle is not easily worked out. When seven-year-old Kevin

"What's the matter? Didn't the prayer from breakfast take?"

reads the passage of Scripture for the family, this may be just the thing to hold his interest. But his stumbling along may not keep his fourteen-year-old brother Larry on the edge of his seat. Yet, there may be ways to get everyone involved. Ask questions and let them ask questions. Share the reading when possible and assign different parts to different members of the family.

8. *Permit spontaneity and make devotions relational.* Our relating to God can also occasion some relating to one another. Devotion time can provoke in-depth sharing if we aim for it. Try asking personal questions—"How did the reading of this passage make you feel?" "How would you have handled this problem?" "David failed here; can you share a time when

you failed? How did you feel?" Relate to the theme; if someone was depressed, ask, "Have you ever been depressed?"

You can also evaluate and affirm each other. If you are looking at a list of the fruit of the Spirit—love, joy, peace, longsuffering, patience, self-control, etc., perhaps you can ask each to tell what fruit they most see in another. This is a great time of affirmation. Then, you can share personal requests for prayer. "Which of these traits do you wish you had more of?" (A hint: use a bowl of fruit when you talk about this. An object lesson keeps their attention longer.) One of the best guides for relational times is *The Serendipity Bible Study Book*.[2]

9. *Be creative and put some variety into what you do.* The worst method is the one you use all the time; methods need to be different if they are to hold interest.

POWER ACTIONS

When you close this book, plan to look for some kind of devotional book, storybook, or object lesson for the kids. For resources, try the Christian bookstore, church library, or the pastoral staff of your church. Before you buy a book, talk to your wife. She may already have something.

Once you have the material, don't announce, "We're having a family altar now!" The only story about an altar they might know is Abraham almost sacrificing Isaac. If you demand their attention, you'll be the one getting burned. Talk to your family and pick out a time to joyfully come together. After that first lesson, discuss how often you should have devotions. Be sure that you've won them over before you push the idea of a "family altar."

COMPETENT TRAINER

PART FIVE

"OK, what did you kids do now?"

TWENTY-ONE

OBSERVE THE GUIDELINES

Discipline As You Are Disciplined

POWER VERSE

The Lord disciplines those he loves....God is treating you as sons. For what son is not disciplined by his father?

HEBREWS 12:6-7

POWER LESSON

"Wait until your father gets home!" This used to be a mom's favorite threat, but it's not as fashionable anymore. We've wised up. Now we believe kids should look forward to Dad's popping through the door. Promising them a spanking for their misbehavior de jour is a sure way to put the damper on seeing him.

Now, Mom has to be an on-the-spot disciplinarian, but Dad should also be involved. The Bible says God the Father disciplines his children, and our Father who is in heaven is a reliable example to fathers on earth. "The Lord disciplines those he loves" (Heb 12:6). This passage takes for granted that dads should do the same. "For what son is not disciplined by his father? If you are not disciplined (and everyone undergoes discipline), then you are illegitimate children and not true sons" (vv. 7-8). This passage sets the standard for discipline.

Teaching with Love

The Bible stresses that learning, not hurting, should be the end product of discipline. The numerous mentions of the "rod of discipline" in the Book of Proverbs might make us think otherwise, since this suggests a painful punishment. In fact one proverb warns parents, "He who spares the rod hates his son" (Prv 13:24).

Yet, Scripture emphasizing discipline is primarily teaching. In fact, the Hebrew word *musar* is sometimes translated "to teach," and other times "to discipline." Discipline should make your child wise: "The rod of correction imparts wisdom, but a child left to itself disgraces his mother" (Prv 29:15). And one of its major lessons is self-discipline. "Listen to your father.... Get wisdom, discipline and understanding" (Prv 23:22, 23). Discipline that hurts but doesn't teach isn't authentic discipline.

Discipline is primarily for our kids' sake, not ours. It's not a way to get our anger off our chest or to make life easier for us, though these might be legitimate by-products. So the kids are noisy when you and your wife want quiet. Getting them to settle down will be good for you. But more than that, your action to get them calmed down should be done to teach them not to interfere with other people.

Because discipline is for the child's benefit, it is a major expression of love. That's what's behind the proverb, "He who spares the rod hates his son." Kids need discipline; to fail to give it to them is unloving. When we need it, God disciplines us. "The Lord disciplines those he loves" (Heb 12:6). This is not a threat but a promise. God will keep us in line because he's a faithful father, not a vengeful one. And, following his example, we should do the same.

We should try to communicate to our kids, "This is for you, not because I dislike you or am angry with you, but because I love you." Not that a kid will always get the message. Thus the joke: "I'm doing this because I love you," said the dad. "Yes, I know," said the son. "I'm sorry I'm not big enough to return your love."

Discipline isn't fun, and it will often seem unfair and unnecessary. Yet, we should try to get our kids to understand what God is trying to get us to understand when he disciplines us: that it's necessary and that it will produce some positive results. "No discipline seems pleasant at the time, but painful. Later on, however, it produces a harvest of righteousness and peace for those who have been trained by it" (Heb 12:11).

The kind of discipline a child receives should be guaranteed not to harm him, even though it may hurt. Paul warned fathers about improper discipline. "Fathers, do not exasperate your children" (Eph 6:4). "Fathers, do not embitter your children" (Col 3:21). If you are overbearing and unreasonable, you may make your child rebel or have little self-respect or "become discouraged" (Col 3:21). Paul strongly urges us to constantly keep in mind the psychological welfare of the child.

D = C + S

Influential psychologist James Dobson constantly reminds parents that kids need control and love. A good attitude needs to be joined with proper technique. In fact, a formula for good discipline would look like this: D=C+S. Discipline equals control and support.

Some experts call parents who offer a child both control and emotional support *authoritative* parents. This is opposite of three other types: the *neglectful,* the *permissive,* and the *authoritarian.* Test yourself to see which type you are by marking what you most typically say to your child. After that, I'll tell you how to score it.

Test Your Discipline Style

1. You need your sleep. To bed! No arguments.
2. Rules are rules. You're late to dinner. To bed without eating!
3. You're late again to dinner, tiger. How can we work this out?
4. Well, you can stay up this time. I know you like this program.
5. Work it out yourself. I'm busy.
6. I won't stand for your back talk. Apologies or Whack!!
7. You can't get up because you kids wanted to stay out past ten o'clock? That's your problem. I've got to get to work.
8. Good grief! Can't you be more careful?
9. Hey, I wish I could let you stay up, but I don't feel good about you missing your sleep.
10. Late again, huh? Pass the meat, please.
11. When we both cool off, we'd better have a talk about this.
12. You're tired, aren't you? A paper route is a tough job. Sure, I'll take you around.
13. You didn't hear me call for dinner? Well, sit down; I don't want you eating cold food.

14. So you think I'm stupid, huh? That's your problem. Beat it.
15. You're really stuck, aren't you? Well, I'll bail you out this time, and then let's figure a better way for the future.
16. Please don't be angry with me; you're making a scene.
17. I don't have to give you reasons. Just do as I say.
18. No son of mine is going to goof off. You took the job. You get it done.
19. You say all the other girls are going to the party? I'd like to have more information before I say yes or no.
20. Jimmy, please try to hurry; Dad will be late if we don't start soon.

If you marked mainly 1, 2, 6, 17, and 18, your style is *authoritarian*. You have a good tone of control, but you don't offer any support. You're tough but not kind. If you marked mostly 5, 7, 8, 10, and 14, you are *neglectful*. You offer neither control or support. If statements you make are like 4, 12, 13, 16, and 20, you are a *permissive* parent. You are high on support, but you offer your kid little or no control. If you marked mainly 3, 9, 11, 15, and 19, you are *authoritative;* that is, you give your kid needed control, but you temper it with a strong display of support.

Studies show that this last type of parenting produces the best results; kids have better self-discipline along with greater self-respect. It's not hard to see why. Their parents' training, though often tough, makes them feel understood and loved. Does yours?

POWER ACTIONS

How do you move in the direction of good discipline? First, figure out your style and analyze it. See where it differs from the authoritative one. Next, decide what steps you need to take to reach your goal. One of the best ways is to role play. The next time you are in the car by yourself, turn off the radio and ask yourself, "What would I do in these situations?"

You caught your child in a lie.

He disobeyed your request to clean his room.

A note from the teacher says he is a distraction in class.

You caught her smoking.

You found him playing with matches.

She rode her bike into a busy street without looking.

I'm sure that you can come up with many more scenarios. In fact, use some of the ones you've experienced. Rehearse how you could have handled it. Actually say to yourself what you should have said to your child. This will help when you face the situation again—you'll feel like you've already been through it once using the right technique. And if someone says, "Hey, I saw you talking to yourself on the way to work today," just answer, "I was disciplining my kids."

TWENTY-TWO

DISCIPLINE BY NATURAL CONSEQUENCES

Enroll Your Kid in the School of Hard Knocks

POWER VERSE

A man reaps what he sows.   GALATIANS 6:7

POWER LESSON

    A few years ago, an accident on our block sent tremors of fear through the neighborhood. An eight-year-old girl lay on the street outside her home, her smashed bicycle beside her and the driver of the car that hit her near panic. Nervous and excited children formed a circle around the injured girl. While they waited for an ambulance, a parent comforted her. Though her injuries turned out to be minor, the impact of the accident was major. For weeks parents noted how no children were carelessly darting from their driveways on the street as they had the day of the accident.

    Like us, children learn that actions can have serious consequences. In this case, they saw what happened to someone else. A kid who darts out on the street on his bike may get hit by a car. Or to put it in the Bible's terms, "A man reaps what he sows."

    Of course, not everyone believes this to the same degree. Some people grow up seemingly oblivious to this simple law of life. They don't seem to appreciate the fact that if you do X, you'll get consequence Y. Famous sayings of irresponsible people are, "I won't get caught," and, "It won't happen to me."

Helping our children make the link between actions and consequences is the major goal of discipline and a prime component of wisdom. This is the gist of the verse, "The rod of correction imparts wisdom" (Prv 29:15). The wise know that wrong acts produce negative results and good ones good results. Therefore, discipline must focus on consequences. There are some practical ways to do this.

Focus on Consequences

1. Expose your kids to the negative things that happen to people who do the wrong things. This complies with the principle of Proverbs 19:25, "Flog a mocker, and the simple will learn prudence." When a simple person (one who is young or naive) sees the public punishment of a mocker (one who scoffs at God and right), he or she will get wise. We learn right from wrong by watching what happens to other people. This, of course, is why the teachers of high school driver training classes show the kids films of traffic accidents. We fathers can do similar things: reading newspaper accounts to them, talking about other people's successes and failures, reading stories and watching videos that show the good guys coming out ahead.

We can also honestly tell them about the price we had to pay for our disobedience or bad decisions. How we respond to God's disciplining us will teach our child how to respond to our disciplining her. "He who heeds discipline shows the way to life, but whoever ignores correction leads others astray" (Prv 10:17). Frequently, I've told my kids about the hard knocks I've received because of my behavior: I sometimes refer

"Hey, Dad? You were right about this unmarked hill. Dad? Are you there, Dad?"

to it as "tuition," the cost of learning a lesson the hard way.

2. *Let your children face negative consequences of their actions and don't always protect them.* Proverbs 19:19 tells what happens to those who shield people from the results of their actions: "A hot-tempered man must pay the penalty; if you rescue him, you will have to do it again." Of course, our children will sometimes need rescuing: we don't let a toddler run out into traffic. But as far as possible, we should let our children face the fallout of their wrongdoing and mistakes. Sometimes it's tough to do, since we can't always discern whether the penalty for some immature action is too severe and we ought to offer protection.

Here's an example of just such a situation. My eight-year-old son had just bought a magic light bulb at a store in our shopping mall. On our way out, walking through the mall, he began taking it out of the box to play with it. I mentioned that it might be a better idea if he didn't do that, since he could easily drop it while he was walking along. He did it anyway and he dropped it. He was shocked and embarrassed as he looked down on the hundreds of pieces of glass.

Not only did he create a difficulty for himself, he also created a dilemma for me. I wondered what I should do. My feeling of frustration wanted to say, "I told you that would happen." My heart wanted to say, "You're only eight and what happened was an accident and you spent all your savings. C'mon, let's go back to the store and I'll buy another one for you." But my mind said, "Stick with the principle of sowing and reaping. He'll miss a valuable lesson if you cough up the dough for him. It's his problem; let him handle it."

I listened to my mind and expressed what was in my heart, saying, "I'm so sorry, Howie. What do you think you should do?"

He used his head, too. "Do you think they'll give me another one if I take this back, Dad?"

At this point, I resisted the urge to tell him he didn't deserve that. "You can go back and ask them if you like." We went back and he asked.

"Where were you when you dropped it?" the clerk asked.

"Right before going through the revolving doors," Howie replied.

"You're lucky," she said. "Our policy is that if you break something while you're still in the shopping center, we'll replace it for you."

She did. Howie was thrilled. I was relieved—I didn't have to play tough.

Many overprotective parents deprive children of what circumstances might have taught them. Scripture seems to say that God is behind those negative circumstances and disciplines us through hard times. We can assume he is also doing the same with our children. By showing too much pity, we can cancel what God is trying to teach them instead of fortifying it.

There are times we should allow a child to make a bad choice or do the wrong thing so that the negative results can teach them. For example, we can let them buy a cheap toy we know is going to break soon after they get it home and allow them to learn something about how to spend their money. And we should resist always warning them and then saying, "I told you so." We need to free them to learn for themselves.

3. Permit natural consequences to teach them. Training our kids would be easy if every time they misbehaved something bad happened. We could simply stand by and watch them learn. But life isn't like that. A child can dash across a street or steal something without suffering any bad results. At times, permitting natural consequences to teach will not be possible. They might be too dangerous or too long-range for our kids to see them coming, such as failing his school subjects. Sometimes it's even tough for them to see the negative results—what junk food, drugs, or smoking can do to the body.

4. Produce negative consequences. Parents must then do more than permit consequences to happen; they have to make them happen. A dad should have a complete stock of negative consequences. They come in two varieties: deprivation (no roller-blading today) or banishment (three minutes alone in the bedroom, especially useful for preschoolers, or a longer time in the bedroom for older children). You simply say, "Behaving as you are, you should not be around the rest of us. Go to your room, and when you choose to behave properly, come on back; we'll be glad to have you."

These will be most effective if we can make the consequences "logical." That is, we should connect the negative result as closely to the misbehavior as possible. If a child writes on the wall, we don't send him to his room, since deprivation doesn't logically result from scribbling graffiti. However, washing it off does. So, we give him a sponge and a bucket of cleaning solution and say, "Scrub." No doubt, he would have preferred being sent to his room. The idea here is that we want our techniques to resemble real life as much as possible, since that's what we are trying to prepare a child for. Sometimes we can even do a bit of overcorrecting; if a kid defiantly spits on the floor, he scrubs the whole floor.

Even though it isn't always possible to logically link the negatives to actions, we should try to do so and communicate this to the kids. "Because your school grades are falling since you learned to drive and you have been running around neglecting your homework, you can use the car only one night a week until your grades improve."

Training Close to Home

Training children to be responsible for doing their chores or hanging up their coats and the like is the most difficult kind of training. Too often, parents train them to do these things only when they are reminded. For example, your kid leaves her school books on the kitchen table instead of in her room as she was told to do. Now, you see them and tell her to take them to her room. She'll do it. But you need to look at the sequence of events to see what is happening. First, school books are left in the kitchen; second, you or your wife see them; third, daughter is told to put them upstairs; fourth, she does as she is reminded. That's the problem. *She does as she was reminded, not as she was told.* This provokes you to say the six most often spoken household words, "I've told you a thousand times!" The key is to get yourself out of the picture and train her to put them in her room when she comes in the door after school.

Training them to do their chores is the same sort of problem. Sure, a son will make his bed after being told by a parent. But the difficulty is getting him to do it without being constantly told.

OK. I've given you enough examples. Now you're waiting for me to tell you how to solve this problem.

The creators of a national parent training program have just the technique for this.[1] Whenever a child leaves something undone, such as making a bed, he is required to pay whoever does it for him. For example, if a child leaves his coat on the living room chair, a brother or sister may hang it up for him and then receive a small stipend for doing so, say twenty cents. The family decides together what the rates will be and the parents enforce the system. Mom and dad also come under the system. Accounts are kept, and each one must pay up at the end of the week.

The payment is not a deduction from allowance. It is important to stress that what is being done is not a punishment but a payment. The kid is learning that in life you must pay for services rendered, and that if you fail to do a job that needs to be done, someone else will have to do it. If he tosses pop cans and hamburger wrappers out of the window, someone has to clean them up. Thus, this procedure fits the qualification of logical consequences. It takes a bit of effort to put the program in place, but we found it was worth it. The kids thought it was fun and it was quite effective, at least until my daughter was old enough to make some money. Then she was happy to pay anyone to make her bed for fifty cents. Not every training system fits all kids at all times. That's why parents should have more than one plan.

POWER ACTIONS

Think back to a situation where you learned from the consequences of your action. Is it a story you can tell your kids? If so, bring it up at dinner time. Then ask them to tell a story about learning a lesson that way. Ask if it is better to learn by experience or by the instructions of someone else. Then ask, "Which way do *you* learn the best?" It will cause them to look for lessons when they get to the painful end of a situation.

TWENTY-THREE
USE BEHAVIOR MODIFICATION
A Positive Approach to the Negative

POWER VERSE
My son, keep your father's commands and do not forsake your mother's teaching.... For these commands... are the way to life.   PROVERBS 6:20, 23

POWER LESSON
My wife and I were enjoying an uninterrupted conversation on a quiet summer Sunday afternoon. Suddenly, I was struck by how unusual that was. With two young kids to care for, Ginger and I rarely had two quiet hours together—at least, not back to back. This time it happened because my son and daughter had been playing outside in the yard for an unusually long time. They were simply being good kids; there was no quarreling or misbehavior to intrude on our peaceful afternoon. After noticing this, I said to my wife, "I'm going to reward them." With a tray of cookies and a pitcher of Kool-Aid in hand, I sat down beside them. "You've been so good this afternoon, Mom and I have had a great time together. For that I have a treat for you." Then we had a party.

As a dad I was practicing what is known as behavior modification. Before I explain how to do it, I'd better defend the practice, since you may have heard some people criticize it. True, this is a term that modern psychologists have invented, especially "behavioral scientists." For that reason, some Christians have rejected it.

My approach is to reject some of what they espouse, but not all. I don't accept their idea that everything people do is simply because they are rewarded or punished for it. And these behaviorists do mean everything, not just our working or playing. Loving, believing, praying—anything we think, feel, or do is simply due to our conditioning.

But I do believe that rewards and punishment motivate and shape some human behavior. This is especially true of kids. Studies reveal that positive or negative consequences play a big part in molding them. Even God uses these to shape us. Not only does he promise to let circumstances knock us around a bit, but he also holds out rewards for serving him. Even Jesus had his eye on some future good when he died for us. He "endured the cross," Hebrews 12:2 explains, "for the joy set before him."

Essentially, behaviorists are describing the old "carrot and stick" approach to discipline, and they especially recommend the carrot. Even that idea isn't new. Tertullian, a Christian theologian from the third century, wrote, "It is better to keep children to their duty by a sense of honor and by kindness, than by fear and punishment."[1]

It's easy to get the mistaken idea that the Bible ignores the carrot approach, but it obviously doesn't. The Proverbs not only threaten that those who misbehave should be punished; they also promise joy and blessing to those who do good. "Esteem her [wisdom], and she will exalt you; embrace her, and she will honor you" (Prv 4:8). "With me [wisdom] are riches and honor, enduring wealth and prosperity. My fruit is better than fine gold; what I yield surpasses choice silver" (8:18-19). Those who follow wisdom and do right will have life (8:35), joy (10:28), and length of life (10:27). They will receive favor from the Lord (8:35) and have the satisfaction of pleasing God: "The Lord abhors dishonest scales, but accurate weights are his delight" (11:1).

God promises plenty to those who walk in his ways. It is not that we earn these things; they are all tokens of grace, but promised, nonetheless. And they affect some of our behavior, but not all. We are also asked to do things sacrificially, for the sake of others. That's where behavioristic theory falls short; it's too simple an explanation for complex human behavior. But it does explain some human behavior, and it gives us some guidance for shaping our kids, especially during their preteen years.

Try Some Behavior Modification

Identify any unwanted, negative behavior, but be sure you're not needlessly forcing change on your child that is not for his own good. To do this right, you have to be quite specific; you can't just conclude he's being bad. Avoid generalizations. You need to be exact. If the child jumps on the couch, you perhaps say, "He's unmanageable," or, "He never listens." Instead, get specific. Say, "He's jumping on the couch and that's not what he should be doing." That way you'll be able to deal with it; it's confusing to deal with an unmanageable child. It's easier to focus on something specific, like stopping your kid from turning the couch into a trampoline.

Now you have to get positive. Ask, "What should my child be doing (a good behavior) instead of doing what he is (a misbehavior)?" Following our example, ask, "What's the opposite of jumping on the couch?" The answer, "Staying on the floor." There are two big reasons for these questions. First, they keep us from always focusing on bad conduct. Sometimes children think that's the only time mom and dad really give

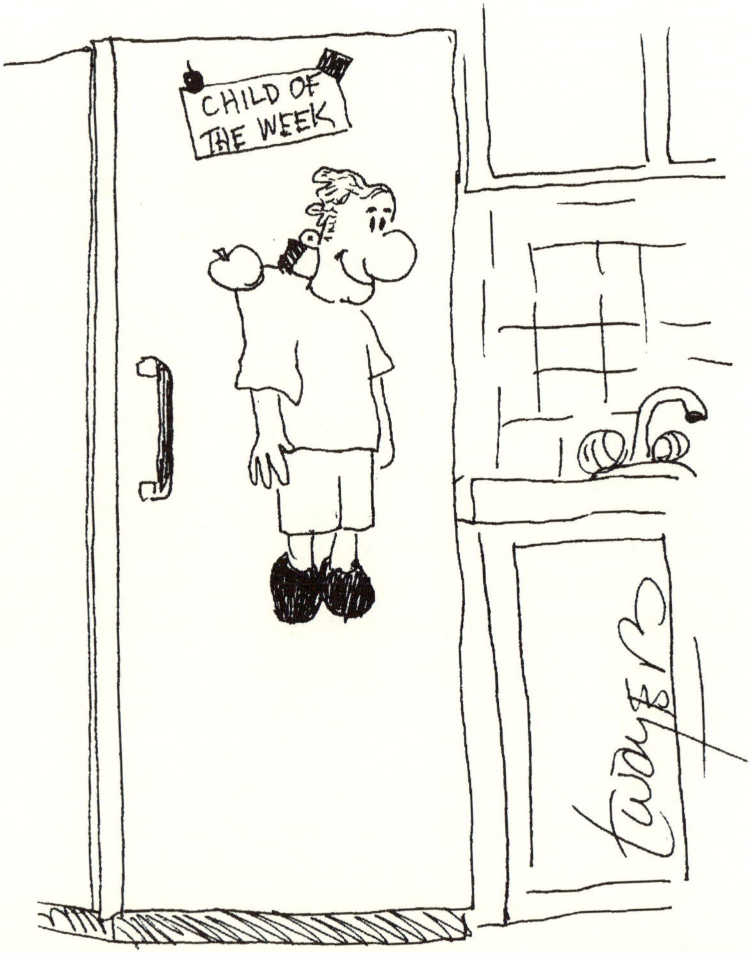
CHILD OF
THE WEEK

them the time of day. Because kids crave attention as much as a Big Mac, they'll even hop on the furniture to be noticed. One of the good features of behaviorism is that it helps us pay attention to good conduct.

Another major reason is that it's easier for anyone to do something than it is to stop doing something. In other terms, it's simpler for your kid to learn to keep his feet on the floor than it is for him to stop jumping on the couch. Perhaps the reason for this is that when you keep yelling, "Don't jump on the couch," it'll ring in his ears, reminding him and tempting him. Instead, get ready to help him do what he should be doing.

Now, you're ready for the next step, which is to ignore the undesirable behavior. When he jumps on the couch, don't mention it. This is tough, because we're so used to thinking about what people shouldn't be doing instead of what they should. And this is especially true of those who feel compelled to come down with both feet on all wrongs. "My kid's vaulting himself off the cushions and I look the other way?" "My daughter eats just a few green beans and I don't remind her to eat them all?" Keep in mind, I'm not suggesting you always discipline this way. Some things you can't and shouldn't ignore. Behavior modification is especially effective when talking or other forms of correction have failed.

The reason for not scolding the child for his bad conduct is to set you up for the next step: to watch for a time when your child is doing the opposite of the misbehavior and then reward him. Recall what we mentioned earlier about your child learning better if you stress what he should do, rather than what he shouldn't. It's easier for him to keep his Nikes on the carpet than it is to keep them off the upholstery. So, to help him, you are going to notice in a big way that he is staying on the floor.

Instead of "catching" him being bad, "catch" him being good and then reward him. This is what I did when I had that Kool-Aid party with my kids, because they were being so angelic. My reward was threefold: my attention, a bit of praise, and food. Any positive response is possible; a reward doesn't always have to be material. There are all types, and knowing what to give when is a bit tricky.

This step, like the third, can look a little odd. As one parent said, "I find it hard to praise a child for small decreases in bad behavior you think should never occur at all, particularly because it sounds so silly. But I'm learning to say, 'Gee, Dan, I don't think you've bitten Michael in two whole days—that's great'; and, 'Look at that: you asked for an apple and you ate almost half of it all up.'"[2] Yet, behavior modification makes sense. Try it.

You'll be doing what one wise parent did, reminding his child, "My son, keep your father's commands and do not forsake your mother's teaching.... For these commands... are the way to life" (Prv 6:20, 23).

POWER ACTIONS

We've probably given you enough action steps in the lesson. Before you can apply any of these, you need to assess how you already are modifying your child's behavior. Take a sheet of paper and draw three columns. At the top of the first write—*Situation*. At the top of the second write—*How I handled it*. And at the top of the third—*How I should have handled it in a positive way*.

Come up with at least five discipline situations that arise with your children. Assess those five. This exercise will help you think of positive ways to approach behavior modification.

TWENTY-FOUR

CONSIDER SPANKING

Does the Carrot Make the Stick Obsolete?

POWER VERSE

He who spares the rod hates his son, but he who loves him is careful to discipline him.   PROVERBS 13:24

POWER LESSON

To spank or not to spank—that is a major question. Experts are not at all agreed on the answer. Some say, "Don't do it," and give a number of reasons. First, there are plenty of other negative consequences to lay on a child. Second, positive rewards are more powerful than punishment. Studies of human behavior seem to confirm this. As a motivator, the carrot is better than the stick. Third, corporal punishment may cause a child physical and mental pain which interferes with a good relationship between parent and child. Fourth, spanking may cause a child to think that hitting others is a way to resolve conflict: "Since Dad hit me, I'll whack you."

Fifth, spanking could easily be abusive. Not all who discourage spanking think it's abusive, but they maintain that if it's done regularly and carelessly, it could lead to abuse. A father, accustomed to hitting his kid, might thoughtlessly do it too hard. Or he might impulsively strike out when angry, perhaps with a hammer in his hand. For these reasons, the Swedish government has made spanking illegal, prosecuting parents who practice it. Their logic is that if they stop the spanking they can reduce the risk of seriously hurting children. The polls now show that the great majority of Swedes support the prohibition. In the U.S., however, research indicates that a majority of parents still consider spanking a legitimate form of discipline.

And many child development experts seem to agree that some forms of negative discipline are OK, even spanking. When the toddler is headed for a busy street, for example, that is not the time to talk.

This leaves us with a conundrum; the Bible seems clearly to be on the side of those who advocate spanking. In the Hebrews passage about God disciplining us, the author refers to a verse from Proverbs which clearly refers to physical punishment, "The Lord... punishes [meaning, beats severely] everyone he accepts as a son" (Heb 12:6).

Some Christians try to dismiss spanking by claiming that the rod mentioned in Proverbs really refers to a shepherd's crook, used not to hit but to rescue. Good try, but that description of the rod doesn't fit the way the word is used, since it's clearly linked to punishment, "Do not withhold discipline from a child; if you punish him with the rod, he will not die" (Prv 23:13).

Another way to discredit such proverbs is to claim they are only for the Old Testament era. Nowhere in the New Testament is spanking specifically recommended. Yet, there is no good reason for ignoring these Old Testament passages. When the writer of Hebrews takes the Proverbs type of discipline for God's style, he seems to endorse it for parents, at least in an offhanded way. God's example is that "he punishes everyone he accepts as a son" (Heb 12:6).

I suggest we take a moderate position on spanking, accepting it as one way of disciplining but limiting its use.

Scriptures portray the benefits of spanking, even speaking rather highly of it as the loving thing to do: "He who spares the rod hates his son, but he who loves him is careful to discipline him" (Prv 13:24). And, "The rod of correction imparts wisdom" (Prv 29:15). Wise people know doing wrong can be harmful.

From a practical point of view, my wife and I have found that spanking often settles a matter much more quickly than other negative consequences. It's done and over with, and the

"Dad, if you're doing this because you love me, I'd rather get flowers."

tense atmosphere between parent and child is quickly cleared. Isolating a child or depriving privileges can drag on for some time. And often it creates more stress for the parent who has to remind the child day after day (if the deprivation extends to a week, for example) that she's banned from something, such as riding her bike.

Yet, despite the benefits, we should spank very cautiously, reserving it for young children. Parents should be careful not to practice a form of discipline that is frowned on by the child's peers and the community at large, and spanking teenagers fits into that category. In fact, spanking isn't fashionable for kids much over seven. By that time they can think logically and parents can better reason with them and use other forms of discipline.

It is extremely embarrassing to kids to undergo a form of discipline they are ashamed to admit. In the past, our communities strongly supported spanking older children. Then a kid, after getting one, would unashamedly say, "I got whacked yesterday for what I did." He might even have been proud his dad cared enough to take him to the woodshed. Today, that's not going to happen, but teens do feel free to talk about more socially accepted disciplinary measures, being grounded, for example.

Paul's warning not to do something that will discourage or exasperate a child applies here (see Colossians 3:21; Ephesians 6:4). Spanking could shame your child and make her turn against you instead of respect you. It is not that the whole neighborhood has to agree with your approach to discipline. But there should be some group to which you belong that does, your church, for example.

How and When to Spank

Don't spank in anger. No punishment should be linked to rage or bitterness. Studies show that children subjected to such an atmosphere have emotional problems. Exclusive use of corporal punishment, particularly in a cool or negative emotional atmosphere, is a wrong use of father power. It communicates hatred more than love. Severe physical whipping and verbal assaults are all too common in America. Give yourself some time to cool off before you spank.

Spanking should be done only occasionally. We must avoid teaching children that the use of force is the primary way to resolve conflict. Use it as a last resort and only when other means cannot be used or have failed. When our kids were little, Ginger and I used to carry a board in the trunk of our car. We traveled a lot as a family, and we wanted it to be a pleasant experience for everyone. Spanking seemed to make sense while on the road, since other forms of discipline were simply not workable. You can't isolate a kid in a Ford—there's no place to send him, and he knows this. When parents are at a disadvantage, kids test them. In our travels, we used that board only a couple of times. Usually, just mentioning our stopping and getting it out of the trunk was enough to straighten them up. However, the threat was a small part of managing the kids on our trips. We tried to make our trips fun, passing out treats, reading aloud, and playing games. Now grown, our kids often refer to the great times we had in the car.

When you spank, do it carefully, avoiding any chance of injuring your child. There's no need for it to hurt a lot. Just the idea of it is enough for most children. Some people recommend using your hand because it is less likely to harm than an object like a stick or hairbrush. However, there are good reasons for using something other than your hand. You want your child to welcome the touch of your hands. Using a stick to spank may keep him from associating your hands with punishment. And a stick may keep you from injuring him. People who use their hands to spank sometimes abuse children by striking out at them in a fit of rage. They hit a child in the face or head, the place where they can most likely be harmed. The advantage of always using the same object is that you have to go and get it. This gives you time to cool down and think, preventing you from impulsively slapping your child. Don't get in the habit of using whatever is handy. A wide, thin board is best. Anything narrow and heavy could bruise or otherwise injure your child. I made a board on which I wrote, "Charity Board: for the Needy."

It's crucial that you always talk to your child before spanking him, explaining why he is being paddled. Your goal is to teach, not to get even. *The measure of a good spanking is how much a child learns, not how much he hurts.*

It's also crucial that you reserve spanking for moral wrongs, not for mistakes or accidents. No child should be punished for immature acts, like knocking over a glass of juice or coming home late because he forgot the time. Parents should discipline when the child defies them. If a child flagrantly refuses to obey, hits the parent, shouts, or shows other signs of mutiny, a parent should come out on top of the situation. Even with an unruly child who constantly hits his parents and other adults, Ann Landers claims spanking a child is wrong—it will teach him that might equals right. She misses the point. By disciplining, we are teaching the child that sometimes might enforces right. Any form of discipline suggests that there is someone more powerful than the child in a position of authority. All of us need to learn that lesson; thus, the Bible supports governmental authority to keep people morally in line.

Spanking should be done in private. Giving verbal rebukes or spankings in public makes your child feel ashamed and embarrassed and can lead to serious emotional disturbances. Jesus' rule about doing to others as you would have them do to you is a good guide for disciplining. None of us wants to be scolded in front of others; kids are no different. Even though this should be obvious to parents, many of them still scold, hit, or spank their kids in public, as most any trip to the shopping mall or grocery store will confirm.

Consider a child's temperament when deciding whether to spank. With some children, paddling isn't effective. Kids differ from one another. The Book of Proverbs notes that people respond differently: "A rebuke impresses a man of discernment more than a hundred lashes a fool" (17:10). A child who is loved and consistently getting wiser will probably require less stringent discipline. And some children simply don't respond to physical punishment. I've had parents tell me about preschoolers they spank twenty times a day without any good results. I quickly suggest that it is best to give it up. Such a child probably needs other measures or has some personal problem that should be uncovered. There's a time to stop spanking and see a counselor.

Finally, talk it over with your wife before you practice spanking. You need to present to your kids a united front. This requires some confabs with her so that you concur on all your parenting procedures. Even if you have different ideas, you need to agree to back each other on whichever you decide to practice. Because spanking is an especially sensitive issue, your wife may have good reason for feeling extremely uncomfortable with your doing it. Those who were abused as children may have an aversion to it, either because they don't want to hurt a child as they were hurt, or because they fear losing control if they spank and ending up injuring their child. The purpose of discipline is to let the child know there are consequences to his actions, both negative and positive. Spanking is only one way to do this.

POWER ACTIONS

Do you and your wife have a set of consequences already drawn up for different misbehaviors? Where does spanking fit in? If you use spanking as a discipline, then the question of what "crimes" receive spanking should be settled ahead of time. If your kids know when they will receive a spanking, it might deter them from those activities.

Also, having known consequences will help you and your wife stay on common ground. Here's how you can do this. Make a list of all the general areas of misbehavior like lying, cheating, stealing, disobedience—realizing that each of those areas has its own subcategories. Disobedience in cleaning a room is not as serious as disobedience by going out drinking. With an age range in mind, decide where spanking is to be used. Transgressions not on your list will need to be dealt with on an individual basis.

TWENTY-FIVE

AVOID DOMINATING

Use Your Urge to Control on Yourself

POWER VERSE

A man will leave his father and mother.   GENESIS 2:24

POWER LESSON

Some men are plagued with what could be called a "control syndrome." For example, in the name of "accountability," they insist a wife report regularly about whether she is staying on her diet, following her exercise plan, and having her personal devotions.

They argue that just as they and several of their Christian buddies agree they should help each other grow spiritually by holding each other's feet to the fire, they and their wives should do the same. To such men, I try to explain that a marriage relationship is not the same as a discipling one.

Married people do place demands on one another. The issue is where you place them and how. We have every right to suggest and even insist on changes that are part and parcel of our marital relationship. A husband can insist his wife not flirt with other men, and a wife that her husband not neglect her for his friends.

But men with a severe craving to control don't stop there. They dominate their wives and kids, permitting them little freedom to be themselves. When they say "Jump!" they want their kids to leap, whether they know why or not.

This kind of dad produces one of two kinds of children. One type is *compliant*. Dominated by his parent, this kid simply never learns to think for herself or to have any confidence in her own decisions. She doesn't strengthen her wings simply because dad won't ever let her fly on her own. She grows up always needing someone to tell her what to do. At best, she will drift through life with little gumption and ambition; at worst, she will succumb to some cult, selling her soul to a strong-willed leader who will replace her overbearing father.

The other type is *rebellious*. Bound so tightly by his father's overbearing regulations, he rebels. This is the only way he can get some freedom to be himself, since his dad won't allow him to make any decisions or to go his own way.

The Need to Differentiate

Neither compliant nor rebellious children develop their inborn capacities and personalities; therefore, they are not what God intended for them to be. When I speak to parents, I use colors to explain what I mean. Suppose your family is "red," the color symbolizing the sum total of your family's likes, dislikes, morals, and beliefs. When your child grows up, she will probably be much like you, but not entirely so. That is, your child will probably be a shade of pink or burgundy. Research shows that the majority of children become adults much like their parents, but not in every detail.

Your child will differ from you since she's a unique individual. As she grows, she will need to become her own person, in control of her own destiny. This means she will become more and more separated from her parents' control. Psychologists call this process "differentiation."

"There will be no slacking off this vacation. We are up at 0600 and to the amusement park by 0800..."

Just how distinct from her family she becomes depends in part on the culture she's in. In our democratic society, we encourage individualism much more than countries that strongly pressure individuals to conform to their families and communities. In some societies, children are under the control of their parents until the parents die. No matter what culture, of course, children will individuate to some extent.

Parents should deliberately help their children go through this process of differentiation. Parenting is not forever. Our kids must eventually go their own way. We assume that this is what is meant by a man leaving his father and mother when he marries. In our society, children are free to make their own decisions by their late teens.

Parents who too tightly control won't allow their child to be pink; they insist he be red. For example, their child's being a Christian is not enough for them; he must also be a Baptist like themselves. And he can't choose his own vocation; he must be a doctor as his dad and grandfather were. On and on it goes; the child is subjected to demands to be someone he may not want to be.

When this happens, some children simply choose to be "red." They succumb to the process. This may be the discouraged child Paul talks about (see Colossians 3:21). Their parents' domination has driven out of them any zest for living, since not being allowed to express themselves seriously dampens their spirits.

Outwardly, these kids look good, complying to all their parents' wishes. Yet, deep down they may be bitter and dissatisfied. Psychologists describe them as persons with "identity foreclosure," meaning that they haven't achieved any genuine personal identity. They never fully develop who they are. They have packaged themselves in their parents' identity, not their own. They are prisoners in the jail their parents have built for them. For now, they have stifled their real self, but later in life, that self may scream loudly to get out. Often, this comes in the early thirties or during the so-called midlife crisis of the forties. During these times, people may decide to break out of the boxes other people have built for them and "do their own thing." Many of them explosively express themselves, creating a crisis. Divorces take place in the early thirties at a higher rate than at any other time; incidents of vocational change are also frequent.

One thirty-something woman in a church we once attended shocked us by being unfaithful to her husband. Raised in a Christian home, appearing to be an exemplary believer, she seemed an unlikely candidate for adultery. In the process of trying to restore her to fellowship, the pastor and church board found her in a state of rebellion. She explained that all her life she had been straightjacketed by her parents' wishes. Now she was breaking free.

Some kids rebel much earlier, often in their teens. Bound too tightly, pushed to be red, they choose to be green. Green might be OK if it is within God's will and a true expression of who they are. However, it most often is not. If the child is green because his rigid parents are red, his choice is not an intelligent decision but an emotional reaction—he's green because he wants to be different from his parents. And his choices will often be destructive. He does drugs or joins a cult so as to be unlike a Baptist, or he fails at school to upset his parents.

The problem is that he is different, but he is not "differentiated." In his rebellion he is still controlled by his parents, because it is because of them he is what he is. He is as much a victim of his parents' domination as the child who simply complies.

Causes of the Control Syndrome

There are practical ways to help a child differentiate, and I'll explain those later. For now, the first step out of this "control syndrome" means taking a good look at yourself. You may think you want to control your child because of your child's need to be controlled, when in reality it is because of your need to control.

Examine yourself. People who are obsessive about controlling others usually are that way because of their own childhood backgrounds.

If you had an alcoholic, drug-addicted, workaholic, seriously ill, psychologically troubled parent or otherwise distressed parent, it may explain why you are a control freak. Because of their condition, these types of parents are in charge of their families. A woman with a bad temper, for example, could explode any time to the detriment of everyone else in the family. So family members "walk on eggs," terrified they may do something to provoke her. Thus, they are under her control. But she herself is virtually out of control. So, when the family is dominated by her, the family itself is now out of control. The same is true for the family of the alcoholic, workaholic, and the like.

Children in such families constantly fight to avoid the chaos. They feel they must control the situation as best they can, because they are terrified of what happens when they don't. They actually battle to keep things on an even keel, and of course, they constantly lose the battle.

Children who grow up in such families become obsessed with controlling everyone around them, because that's what they are in the habit of doing. They do it because they have this hidden fear that if they don't, terrible things will happen.

Understanding how you got your "control syndrome," if you have it, will help you recognize it for what it is and then deal with it. Ask yourself, "Am I a control freak?" Then give yourself an honest answer.

POWER ACTIONS

Here's what you do: you gather everyone together and tell them what they must do in order for you to work on your "control freak" attitude. Oops, isn't that just what a control freak would do? Then, let's do something completely different. Here's an action step to take.

For one whole week, ask everyone else what they want to do. If no one says anything, quietly read a book. Suggest nothing. By the third day, someone besides you will suggest an activity. Follow along. Don't try to think of ways to do it better or faster. Just follow along with what is going on.

The next night, there will be more suggestions than you know what to do with. Have the kids work out what to do. Don't jump in unless they are bloodying one another. Once they've decided, follow along. Do that for a whole week. Then suggest an activity, but in a way that leaves the door wide open for the family to do something else instead. Before you know it, you'll be controlling your family less, but enjoying it a whole lot more.

"I told you not to get him that for Christmas."

TWENTY-SIX

HELP YOUR CHILD DIFFERENTIATE

Teach Your Kid to Fly

POWER VERSE

Train a child in the way he should go, and when he is old he will not turn from it. PROVERBS 22:6

POWER LESSON

Getting the young out of the nest, both safe and competent, is a tricky process, even for birds. The female Philippine eagle looks after her eaglet with great care, feeding it regularly until it is strong enough to fend for itself. The big problem the mother faces is knowing when the young bird is able to do it. If she allows it to leave the eyrie before it can make a kill or defend itself, it will either starve to death or be killed by a predator. If she waits too long, the test time for learning to make a kill will have passed. So the process of handing over responsibility to the young bird, and of teaching it to survive in the world, is a delicate one.

For humans, it's even more complex. Grown kids must attain some freedom in three ways: financially, functionally, and emotionally. This involves their making enough money to care for themselves without their parents' help. It also means being able to make decisions and solve problems in a responsible way without always asking mom and dad. Certainly, they should feel free to ask for advice, but they need to act on their own. Breaking the emotional tie is the most difficult of the three. Those adults who are still disastrously shackled to their parents emotionally are most likely to be from a dysfunctional home.[1]

The famous proverb, "Train a child in the way he should go and when he is old he will not depart from it," makes clear a major principle of parenting. We should train children to be independent of us and yet to follow our teaching when they are old. Parents aren't around forever, and kids eventually need to learn to act on their own. In the last chapter I described the need for a child to differentiate from his parents as he grows. Here are some guidelines for helping your child do it successfully.

Helping Your Child Differentiate

Gradually increase your children's freedom to make their own decisions as they grow. You can start early by letting them decide matters that are not moral and that will not put them in danger. Give your kids an allowance and also the freedom to use it. Some parents, when kids seem responsible, include enough in their allowance money to buy their own clothes. Of course, they may prove to be irresponsible, so you take some risks and put them to the test, allowing them to choose for a while. If they mess up, you take the privilege away for a time, always with the idea that later you can let them try again to prove themselves reliable. It is important to give them freedom to fail.

It's not always easy for parents to know which matters are too risky for children to handle. Decisions about clothes, for example, can have moral implications related to their welfare. A daughter might want to dress in a way that is too sexually provocative, or a son might want a jacket that won't really protect him from the winter weather. In such cases, we can still give them some power to decide, but with conditions.

Even then, the process is not free of risk. Take contemporary music as an example. Some Christians tell parents to forbid their teens to listen to rock music because the rhythm is sinful, or because many of the lyrics are just plain bad. Yet, a blanket restriction of all rock music might do more harm than good. Better to make a few stipulations and try to teach our children to discern for themselves what's good or bad. We do this not only because we are trying to help them make judgments and control themselves in the future, but because even now we can't always be watching over their shoulder. And as children grow older, spending more time away from us, it becomes even more difficult to do so. The father of a fourteen-year-old daughter observed, "I feel that the circle of her life is widening away from us."

Another way to help your kid differentiate is to establish clear boundaries. Draw a circle around your kid, but make sure there's plenty of freedom within it. The boundaries are needed because he's not wise enough to make all decisions, but the freedom is needed because he will learn wisdom from making decisions. Parents should make clear what they expect in regard to drug use, nonmarital sex, and the like.

You should be strict, but wisely choose what you will be strict about. As some experts suggest, "Choose your battles carefully with your children." You want to make sure you maintain control. If you fight over the wrong thing you may end up losing your child's respect and obedience. Consider the matter of regulating what your kid watches on TV. On his radio program James Dobson answered a caller who wanted to know if it was proper to make all TV programs off limits to her children, as her pastor wanted her to do. "Do you mean all

TV—including Sesame Street and other educational programs?" he asked. "Yes," she replied. Dobson answered he wouldn't do that, explaining that if a parent's rules deprive children of their cultural heritage, someday they are going to grow up and throw those rules back in their faces. Dobson is right. You must be sure that in the process of defending your children, you don't deny them what is rightfully theirs. If you do, they may turn against you.

Expect confusion in deciding exactly how much freedom should be given and when. "My thirteen-year-old daughter wants to sleep overnight at a friend's house. Should I permit it?" To answer such questions, consider a number of things.

1. *Does the child need protection in a circumstance she is not able to handle yet?* Spending the night in someone else's home can be threatening. Not all parents are responsible, nor do they all have your values. They might show videos you don't want her to see, or even worse, she might be exposed to some sort of sexual abuse. It's in the child's interest to insist that you know the family. Don't apologize for wanting to meet them and learn something about them before you agree to her request. It helps your child be more safely independent if you have a network of families you know and respect, so that your child can go beyond the family circle.

2. *You should know how your child feels.* Kids in the early teens often want a parent's control, even though they may appear to resent it. They are often afraid of situations that threaten them, and yet they don't like to say no to their peers. They feel relieved when the parents say no for them. Experts say that teens are more secure when the parents create clearly understood boundaries that keep them from harm. It helps them to be able to say, "My dad won't let me."

3. Don't cross over their personal boundaries into areas that are not your business. You must permit your kids to have their own private life and not claim the right to invade that domain at any point. If you secretly search a child's room or read his mail, you will make him feel violated, just as you would. Many parents even declare a child's room his own domain; he is permitted to keep it as he likes. Of course, you can insist the condition of his room not impede the well-being of others in the family. No half-eaten hamburgers, for example, should be left under the bed to putrefy, stink, and attract bugs. There are limits, but these limits should not intrude on a kid's personal space.

This should be true in how your kid spends his spare time, once ordinary responsibilities are cared for. You have to learn to accept his saying no in matters that are strictly personal.

Allow a kid to express his feelings and opinions, and make it safe to disagree without fear of criticism, rejection, or isolation. By this you are saying loud and clear, "We respect you. We encourage you to think for yourself, and we want you to be able to express your feelings in appropriate ways." One man told me he and his wife tried to make this happen in their family by building in a special time for it. Tuesday supper was "complaint time," when they invited their kids to voice any gripes or conflicts they had with mom and dad. Of course, this didn't require the parents to cave in to their kids' view of things, but they did listen; and when they disagreed, they tried to do it agreeably. The message to the kids was, "You have a right to think and express your own thoughts." In cases where the kids' thinking could not change the parents' demands, they still tried to show respect, saying something like, "You have a right to believe such and such is OK, and when you are old enough and we are not responsible for you, you may do as you wish. But right now, we cannot allow you to do what we think is not best for you."

In regard to their feelings, we want children to know that talking about them is always OK. We want them to tell us when they're frustrated, dejected, or angry with us. But we also explain that certain forms of expression are not acceptable: calling people names, hitting, pouting, failing to listen.

Unconditional Love

Children will most closely follow parents who display a combination of teaching, example, and love. In our efforts to discipline, we should not withdraw our love or threaten to do so. Unconditional love becomes an issue particularly in the case of rebellious teenagers. Parents are caught between defending their own morals and expressing their natural affection. In this battle, some parents believe they must stand up for values and reject the child who has left the Christian faith, become a homosexual, or turned into a delinquent. But even in these cases, it seems best not to betray the natural love tie. After a teen builds a wall between himself and his parents, if the parents also build a wall, the two walls must be broken down to create a reconciliation. When parents keep the door of their love open, they continue to influence the child.

Love does not always include giving in to our children, providing money or other support for destructive activities. Love must sometimes be tough and deny propping up someone who continually insists on falling. We can still refuse without rejecting. Like the father of the prodigal son, we can pour out our affection, no matter what far country the child might wander to.

Parents should dose out responsibility insofar as the child shows she is responsible. Disciplining teens, especially, is not a matter of simply laying down the law. There is room for negotiating. David Elkind, one of the major authorities in the field of child development, suggests viewing parent-teen relationships as a series of contracts. The first contract zeros in on this idea of freedom and responsibility. Parents tell the kids they'll have more liberty as they are more trustworthy. "Sure, you can have the family car more since you are doing your homework and you come in on time and you are going to the right places with the right people." Elkind says we give too much freedom to irresponsible kids.

Another contract deals with loyalty and commitment. Here you simply expect your kid to remain loyal to values and beliefs you hold, while, in turn, the teens can count on you to live out those values. "Hey, they're for you, but also for me. You live by them; I will too. I won't force you to hold standards I don't follow."

The third type of contract is related to their attempts to achieve and your support of them. A parent makes it clear, "If I pay for piano lessons, I expect you to practice. It works the other way too: as long as you practice, I'll pay."

Kids need you to negotiate with them because they need to learn how to do so. Being able to negotiate successfully is part of what it means to be mature. And producing mature people is what disciplining is all about.

POWER ACTIONS

Knowing when to release your kids is tricky; teaching them that it is a process is equally difficult. Here are a few suggestions for discussion on the process.

Get a helium balloon, a bird, a turtle, or a kite. Round up the kids and take them out to a field. If it is a kite, wait for a calm day and take the kids out to try to fly the kite. With no wind it will continue to come crashing back to the ground. Tell the kids, "It looks like I tried to let this go at the wrong time. We'd better wait for a windier day." When the windy day hits, take your kids and the kite back to the field. Let that baby soar! Then ask them, "Do you remember when we came out here on the wrong day? What happened to the kite?" Next ask what happened when they waited for the right time. The kite soared.

With a balloon, let it go with a stamped postcard on it. Ask that the card be sent back with the finder's address on it. Watch the balloon float in the air (put a small piece of aluminum foil on the string to catch sun reflections). As it goes into the air, ask where the kids think it will land. Tell them that where it lands depends on when it is let go.

Then let them know that your relationship to them is a lot like that. God has given them to you to care for, and you want to wait for just the right time to allow them to do certain things. These freedoms will grow until someday they are independent.

TWENTY-SEVEN

EMPOWER
Be a Support, Not a Substitute

POWER VERSE

Carry each other's burdens, and in this way you will fulfill the law of Christ.... Each one should carry his own load.

GALATIANS 6:2, 5

POWER LESSON

"Mommy, I can do it!"

"No, I'm gonna teach you. You have to do it my way."

"No, Mommy, let me do it!"

So went the conversation as a mother was trying to teach her three-year-old child how to do something. Just prior to this, she had watched him do the task by himself—and do it rather well. You might have expected her to let him continue. However, this mom simply intruded, took over the task and insisted the child follow her instructions. After two minutes of this "teaching," the three-year-old pushed the task away and said to the mother, "You do it." This child, who initially had worked quite competently alone, had now simply given up.

Incidents like this one told by Cynthia Neal are all too common in our homes.[1] Instead of building up our children's confidence, we do things to tear it down. To have some self-reliance, children need a positive perception of themselves. There are three components to this.

1. *A child should see herself as competent,* able to say, "I am capable." This, of course, should include trust in the Lord; as Christian parents, we're not trying to encourage independence from him. Rather, we're trying to show that God has given her talents and abilities he can enable her to use. She should not have the attitude that she just can't do anything right, with a lifetime membership in the "I can't" club.

2. *A child should perceive herself as having power.* She should be able to look in a mirror and say to herself, "I can influence what happens to me." Again this is not to teach her to pit herself against God's will, as if she is captain of her own soul and master of her fate. We don't teach her she has absolute power; but we do want to make her believe she has some power. Our child needs to be convinced she has some control and is responsible for her choices and actions.

3. *A child should perceive herself as able to relate properly to others,* the inner voice saying, "I contribute in meaningful ways and I am genuinely needed."[2] Otherwise, she will perceive herself as meaningless.

All this adds up to empowering our children to have confidence in themselves and in the Lord. This involves not putting them down but building them up. There's a good word for this: empowering. It means assisting our kids to do their own thing and as far as possible to do the right thing.

Support Your Children

But this means we have to refuse to do for them what they should do for themselves. Too often, we try to fix our kids instead of helping them do it themselves. In effect, we say, "I'll go into the game for you," rather than, "Go for it and I'll stay on the sidelines and cheer." Our kids need supporters, not substitutes. Here's how to be one.

"I don't mind my Mom playing the outfield for me but she's <u>only</u> batting 180."

Refuse to answer every question they ask. Enable them to learn for themselves. Instead of merely giving answers, show them how to find answers.

When helping them solve a problem, suggest options instead of telling them what to do. Say, "I see three alternatives in your situation. Here they are... think them over." Don't always solve their problems for them or tell them what's right or wrong. Teach them how to deal with their own issues and develop their own conscience. As long as you are willing to take their problem, they won't own it themselves. Kids, as well as anyone else, cannot learn to be responsible as long as someone constantly says, "Here, let me do it for you."

It's wrong to try to stop drinking, eating, gambling for another person. You only perpetuate the problem. Sure, the Bible says: "Carry each other's burdens, and in this way you will fulfill the law of Christ" (Gal 6:2). But only a few sentences later it warns, "Each one should carry his own load" (6:5). The different Greek words used for burdens and load explain the difference. Burdens are like rocks too heavy for one person to handle. At times troubles are such that we need others to help by giving us a lift. The load is like a backpack, representing what we ourselves are personally responsible for carrying. When we take someone else's assigned backpack, we rob him of the opportunity to solve his own problem and do his own thing. Love means doing what's best for others. And what is best is doing whatever we can to make them feel responsible for their own lives. It is not in their best interest to make them depend on us to do what they should be doing for themselves.

To try to determine how to respond to your child's problem, you can ask, "Who owns it?" In any situation, try separating your problem from theirs. For example, if your kid is too slow climbing out of bed and getting ready for school, causing him to miss his bus, you all obviously have a distressing situation. Yet, your problems are different. Try to distinguish how it affects each of you. It's a problem to you and/or your wife in that it could mean:

- letting him miss school and making you feel like an irresponsible parent,
- making you miss going to work on time because you wait for him to come down for breakfast,
- causing you the inconvenience of driving him to school.

Now, stop and consider the problem from the kid's point of view. Ask, "How could this be a problem for him?" In other words, what are the consequences for someone who doesn't learn to get up and going in the morning?

- He is going to fail to develop a personal discipline he will need for the rest of his life.
- He might miss breakfast.
- He might have to stay home if he misses the bus, and that could eventually be frustrating.
- He might have to walk to school (if reasonably possible).

After you've figured all this out, you can now devise a plan to deal with it.

- You can yell at him a dozen and a half times each morning till he gets going. But that just makes a problem for you, and it won't help your kid's inner voice to yell at him. As long as you yell for him, why should it?
- You can try some positive reward for the mornings he does crawl out on time.
- You can sit down and have a talk with him about the problem he is causing you. Tell him how this creates troubles for you: the inconvenience, the feelings of concern for him, the worry about his education. It's important to approach the situation from your point of view, not lecturing the kid about himself, but explaining what it's doing to you.

This is a good approach that sometimes works far better than we would suppose. Picture this scenario. A rebellious teen stays out at night long past the hour he is supposed to be home. His father tries everything he knows to get him to obey, but nothing works. One evening, the son slithers in the doorway very late to find the light on in the living room, his father waiting for him. Expecting a lecture or an angry outburst, his dad simply says, "Sit down and we'll talk." Beginning with, "I love you, but I no longer know what to do with you," he explains how discouraged he feels and what problems his son is creating for him in his attempt to be a responsible parent. He ends with, "What do you suppose we should do?" They then talk, and the son's rebellion comes to an end. This can actually happen.

If an honest talk doesn't get the kid hustling in the morning, there is one more approach. You simply let him deal with the problem himself, and then you deal with the problems it's causing you. First, you refuse to wait till he shows for breakfast and instead let him miss it or get his own. Second, if he misses his bus, you no longer drive him to school. He can stay home or walk to school. If these options are too severe, you can make him go to bed earlier until he learns to get up on time. We're applying the principle we discussed earlier, letting the kid face natural consequences and not shielding him. If you let him depend on your outward discipline, he will never develop inner discipline of his own.

Empowering is the essence of fathering. A man recently told a group of us how he came to realize he had not empowered his son as he should have. Even now that his son is grown, he tends to do things for him, rather than supporting him in doing them for himself. "A few weeks ago, he called me for help in fixing his air conditioner," he told us. "Then, after a couple of minutes of trying to explain, I got frustrated and said, 'I'll be right over.'" The father fixed it for his son. He was, essentially, saying to his son, "You can't do this; move over and let me do it."

Then this father explained that now that he was aware of his shortcoming, he was trying to change. He continued, "So, the other day, my son phoned again for help fixing something. This time, I explained how it could be done and then said confidently: 'You can do it.'" At that our little group cheered as if we had just seen him hit a home run. And in a sense, we had.

Power hitters make power hits: Power Dads make power people. Be one. It's never too late to start.

POWER ACTIONS

Set up a night and have each family member write down his or her greatest current problem. Put the papers into a hat. The problems need to be task-oriented, not personal. That makes it easier for the demonstration to work and the lesson to be learned.

Draw the first one and discuss how to solve it, utilizing the correct problem-solving techniques. A caution: do not expect everyone to work the plan in the same way. Some will approach it sequentially and others from outside the box. Just give them the guidelines and don't do it for them! Two things will happen: the kids will learn how to solve problems, and your family will begin the process of bearing one another's burdens. That's a double whammy.

ONE
Realize the Need

1. David Blankenhorn, *Fatherless America: Confronting Our Most Urgent Social Problem* (New York: Basic Books, 1995), 70.
2. Blankenhorn, 26-27.
3. Barbara Whitehead, "Dan Quayle Was Right," *The Atlantic Monthly* (271:4, April 1993), 47.
4. Blankenhorn, 25-48.
5. A. Bell, M. Weinberg, and S. Hammersmith, *Sexual Preference: Its Development in Men and Women* (Bloomington, Ind.: University Press, 1981) in Jack O. and Judith K. Balswick, *The Family: A Christian Perspective on the Contemporary Home* (Grand Rapids, Mich.: Baker, 1989), 188-89.
6. George Alan Rekers, "Psychological Foundations for Rearing Masculine Boys and Feminine Girls," in Wayne Grudem and John Piper, eds., *Recovering Biblical Manhood and Womanhood: A Response to Evangelical Feminism* (Wheaton, Ill.: Crossway, 1991), 298.

TWO
Picture the Role

1. Michael Farquhar, "Pop Was a Weasel," *Chicago Tribune*, 16 June 1996, Section 13, pp. 1, 5.
2. Bob Condor, "Rape," *Chicago Tribune*, 7 January 1996, Section 13, p. 6 (story begins on p. 1 and ends on 6).

THREE
Picture the Role (Part 2)

1. Blankenhorn, 42.
2. Blankenhorn, 215.
3. Blankenhorn, 215.
4. Blankenhorn, 103.
5. Rekers, 299.
6. Rekers, 303.

FOUR
Recognize the Rewards

1. From a commencement speech at Wellesley College, May 1994. Quoted in *On the Father Front*, vol. 8, p. 1.

FIVE
Face Your Fear
1. Ellen Galinsky, *Between Generations* (New York: Time Books, 1981), 229.
2. Merton P. Strommen and A. Irene Strommen, *Five Cries of Parents* (San Francisco: Harper & Row, 1985), 16.

SIX
Be Consistent
1. Ken R. Canfield, *Seven Secrets of Effective Fathers* (Wheaton, Ill.: Tyndale, 1992), 82.
2. Patricia O'Gorman and Philip Oliver-Diaz, *Breaking the Cycle of Addiction* (Deerfield Beach, Fla.: Health Communications, 1987), 32, 33.
3. From the TALMUD: Yoman, 78b. In Rosten's book of quotes. Compendium of twelve hundred years of dialectic, from the fifth century before Christ to the eighth century A.D. Commentary, discussion and debate on the TORAH (first five books of the Old Testament) by over two thousand rabbis.
4. Canfield, 82.
5. Canfield, 91.

SEVEN
Deal with Your Past
1. Richard H. Price and Steven J. Lynn, *Abnormal Psychology in the Human Context* (Homewood, Ill.: Dorsey, 1981), 369.
2. Nancy E. Downing and Margaret E. Walke, "A Psychoeducational Group for Adult Children of Alcoholics," *Journal of Counseling and Development*, April 1987, vol. 65, 440.
3. Barbara Forsstrom-Cohen and Alan Rosenbaum, "The Effect of Parental Marital Violence on Young Adults: An Exploratory Investigation," *Journal of Marriage and the Family*, May 1985, 467.

EIGHT
Tap into the Power Source
1. E. E. LeMasters and John DeFrain, *Parents in Contemporary America, A Sympathetic View* (Belmont, Calif.: Wadsworth Publishing Co., 1983), 1.

2. John Demos, *Past, Present, and Personal: The Family and the Life Course in American History* (New York: Oxford University Press, 1986), 41-67.
3. Norman Vincent Peale, *Favorite Stories of Positive Faith* (Pawling, N.Y.: Foundation for Christian Living, 1974), 16-18.
4. George Whitefield, as quoted in Ray Stedman, *Body Life* (Glendale, Calif.: Regal, 1972), 112.

NINE
Be Always Changing

1. Norman Bell, in a lecture for visiting faculty of Campus Crusade's "Institute of Biblical Studies," summer 1975.

TEN
Manage Anger

1. David Mace, *What Is Happening to Clergy Marriages* (Nashville: Abingdon, 1980), 32.

TWELVE
Plan Your Life

1. R. Alec MacKenzie, *The Time Trap* (New York: Amacom, 1972), 38-39.

THIRTEEN
See the Value of Conversation

1. Samuel Osherson, *Finding Our Fathers* (New York: Free Press, 1985), 1.
2. This account is taken from my book *Unfinished Business: Helping Adult Children Resolve Their Past* (Portland, Ore.: Multnomah, 1988) 13-23.
3. Michael E. McGill, "Family Man Seldom Lives Up to His Name." *Chicago Tribune,* Tuesday, June 18, 1985. Section 5, 4.

FIFTEEN
Learning to Listen

1. Paul Tournier, *To Understand Each Other,* trans. John S. Gilmour (Atlanta, Ga.: John Knox, 1967), 4.

SIXTEEN
Understand How Kids Think
1. Emerson E. Eggerich, "A Descriptive Analysis of Strong Evangelical Fathers," unpublished doctoral dissertation, Michigan State University, East Lansing, Michigan, 1992.

TWENTY
Conduct Family Devotions
1. Ronald Goldman, *Religious Thinking from Childhood to Adolescence* (London: Routledge and Kegan Paul, 1964).
2. Lyman Coleman, Denny Rydberg, Richard Peace and Gary Christopherson, *The Serendipity Bible Study Book* (Grand Rapids, Mich.: Zondervan, 1988).

TWENTY-TWO
Discipline by Natural Consequences
1. *Parent's Handbook of Systematic Training for Effective Parenting*, published by American Guidance Service, Inc., Circle Pines, MN 55104.

TWENTY-THREE
Use Behavior Modification
1. *Encyclopedia of Quotations: A Treasury of Wit and Humor* (Philadelphia: David McKay, 1894), 54.
2. Catherine Caldwell Brown, "It Changed My Life," *Psychology Today*, November 1976, 47.

TWENTY-SIX
Help Your Child Differentiate
1. Timmen L. Cermak and Stephanie Brown, "Interactional Group Therapy with the Adult Children of Alcoholics," *International Journal of Group Psychotherapy*, 32 (3), July, 1982, 377.

TWENTY-SEVEN
Empower

1. Cynthia Jones Neal, *Nurture That Is Christian,* eds. James C. Wilhoit and John M. Dettoni (Wheaton, Ill.: Victor, 1995), 123-24.
2. H. Stephen Glenn and Jane Nelson, *Raising Self-Reliant Children in a Self-Indulgent World; Seven Building Blocks for Developing Capable Young People* (Rocklin, Calif.: Primar), 49-50.